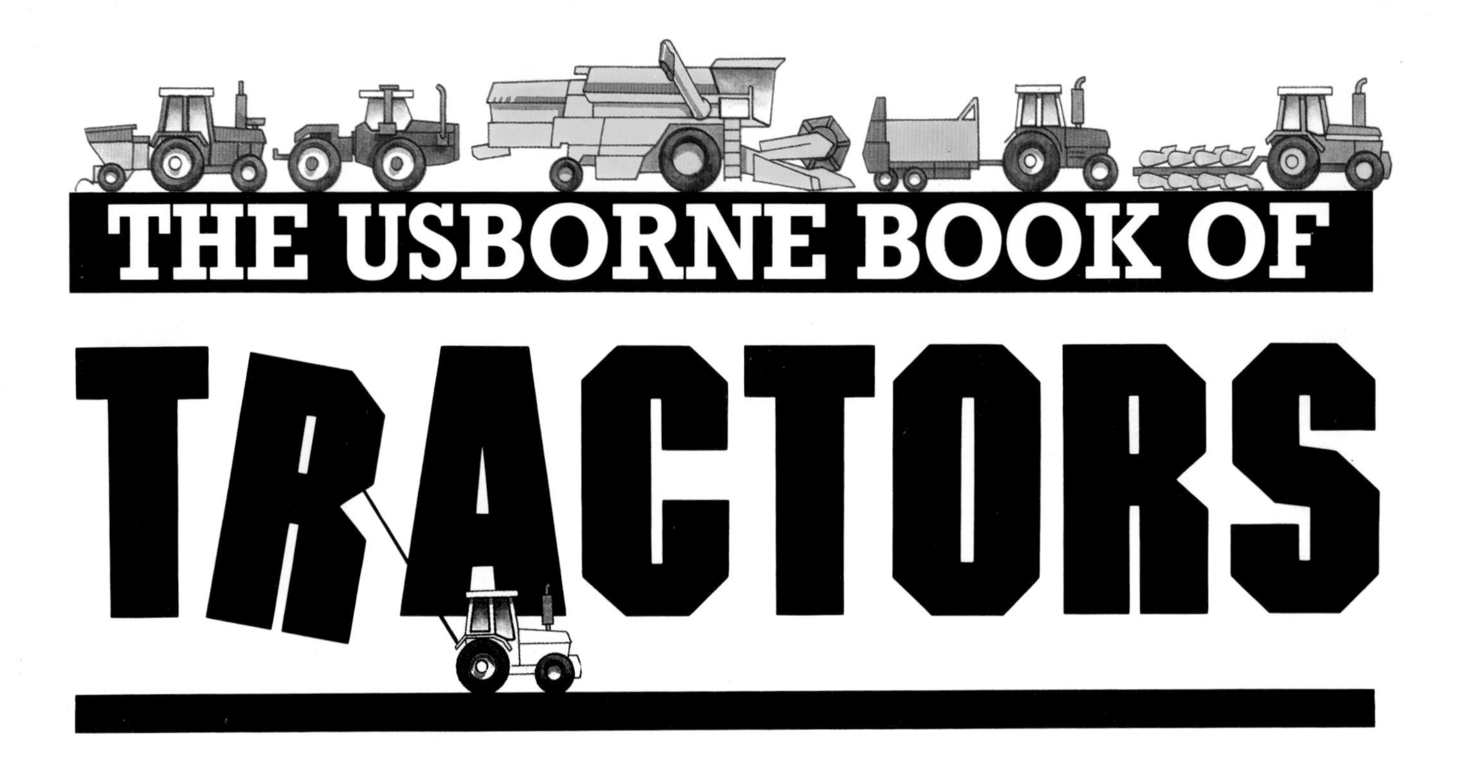

Caroline Young

Designed by Steve Page

Illustrated by Chris Lyon and Teri Gower

Consultant: Mick Roberts (Machinery Editor, Farmers Weekly)

Contents

Tractors

Tractors have to do many different jobs on a farm and can work in all sorts of weather.

Farmers drive them over bumpy, muddy fields, so they have to be tough and hard-wearing.

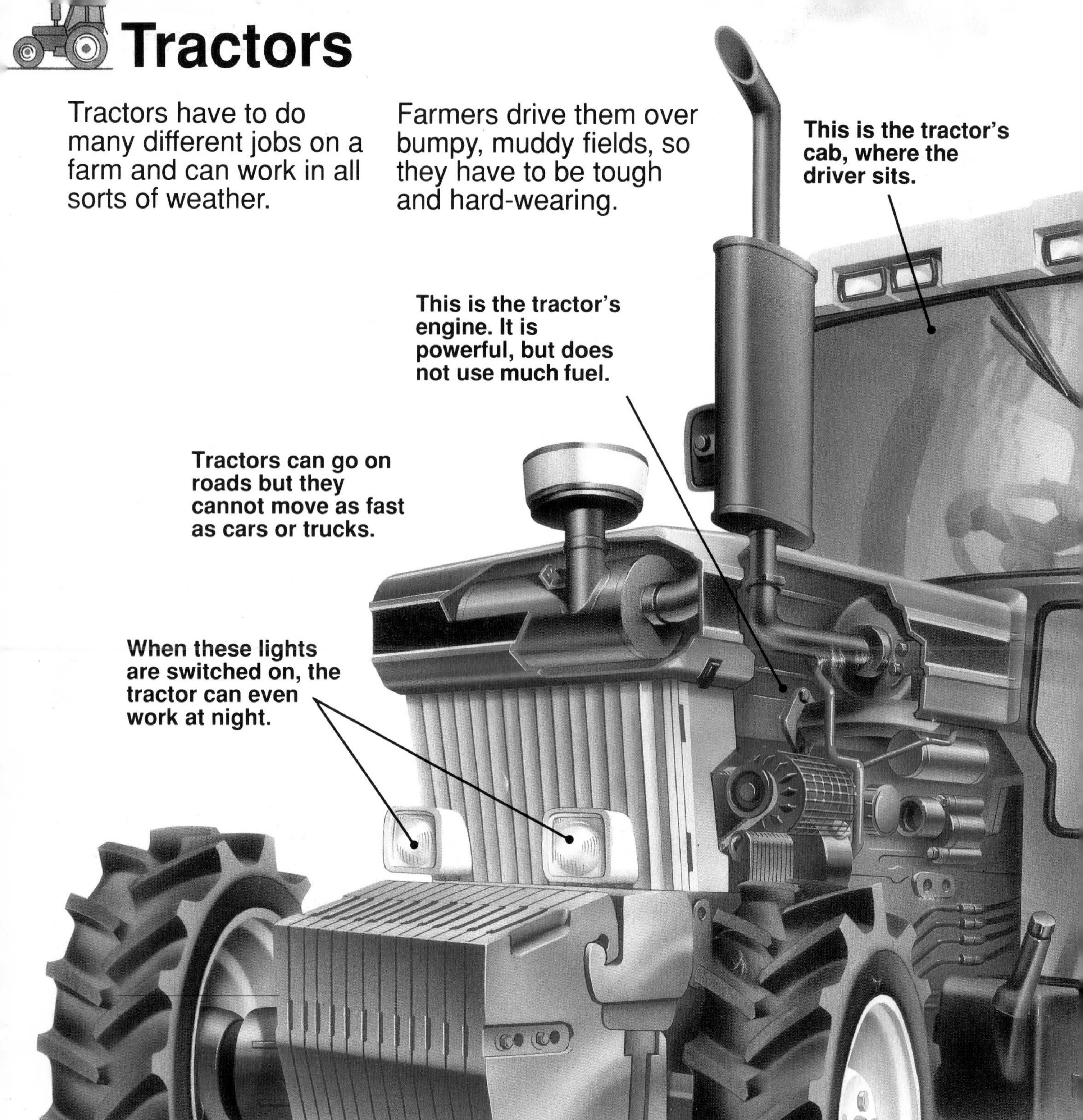

This light flashes when the tractor drives on roads. Other drivers see it and slow down.

This back window opens to let fresh air into the cab in hot weather.

The cab has a heater for cold weather.

Tractors can easily tip over if they drive up very steep slopes. These metal bars stop the farmer from getting crushed if that happens.

Tractors can turn around in small spaces. They must not squash crops in the fields.

Mud and bumps

Tractor tires have deep grooves in them. They grip wet, muddy ground without getting stuck.

A tractor's body is high above the wheels, to stop damage from rocky, bumpy ground.

Its powerful engine keeps the tractor going up any sloping ground around the farm, too.

Three links

Tractors pull many different farming tools behind them.

The tools are fastened to three metal links behind the cab.
A metal pole called a Power Take-Off (P.T.O.) carries power from the tractor's engine to the tools. This makes them work.

Tractors at work

A tractor's main job is driving up and down fields, pulling farming tools. The four tools on this page get the ground ready for crops to grow.

Plow

This tractor is pulling a plow. Plows break up and turn over hard, flat earth. They also bury weeds. This makes the ground better for planting seeds in.

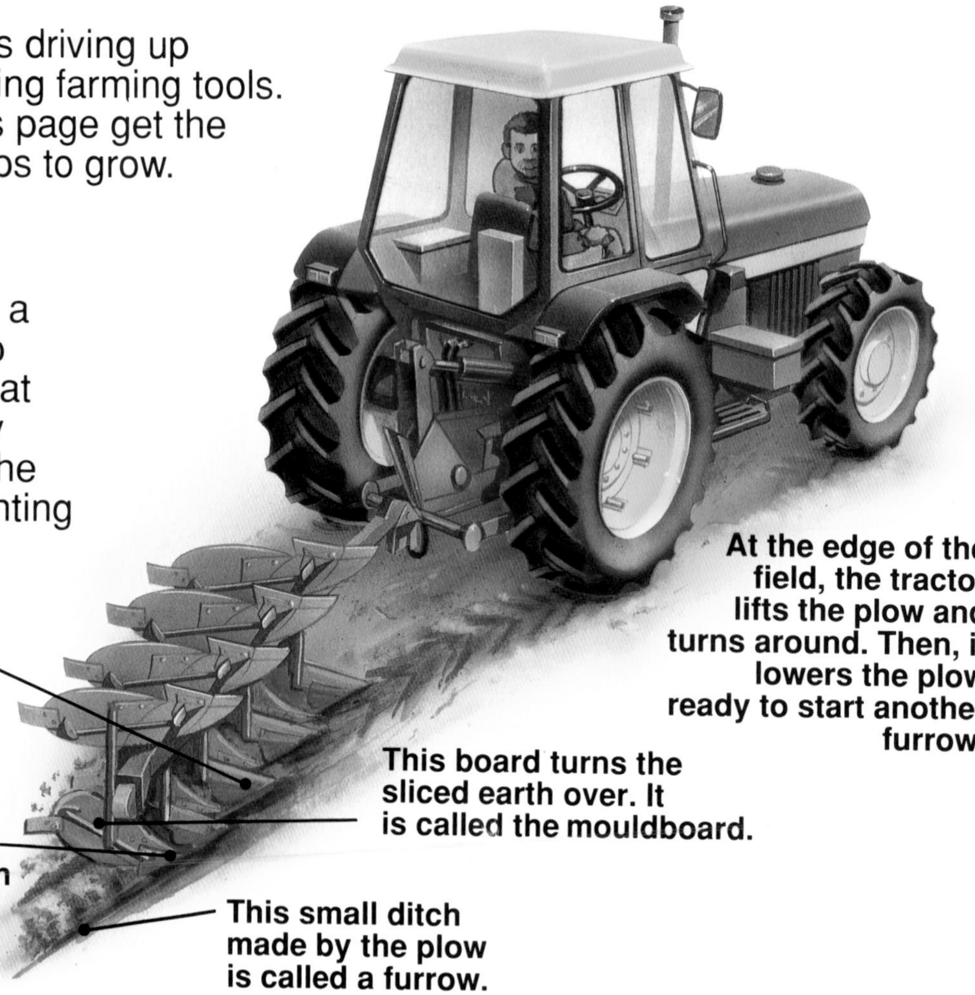

At the edge of the field, the tractor lifts the plow and turns around. Then, it lowers the plow ready to start another furrow.

Metal blades called coulters cut straight down into the ground.

This board turns the sliced earth over. It is called the mouldboard.

These blades are called shares. They slice under the earth cut by the coulters.

This small ditch made by the plow is called a furrow.

Harrow

This tractor is pulling a harrow. Harrowing breaks down the big slices of earth the plow has made.

These rows of metal discs break down clods of earth as they are pulled over it.

This harrow has over 35 discs. They are arranged in rows called gangs.

Gang

This type of harrow is called a disc harrow.

The gangs are spread out behind the tractor to harrow more earth.

This metal bar is called a shaft. The harrow's discs are attached to it.

Roller

This roller smooths the earth after harrowing. It makes the field level for planting seeds in.

Each of these rollers is made up of 20 steel rings.

A tractor can roll a field quickly with wide rollers. It has to make fewer trips up and down it.

Stones can damage farm machines. The rollers press them into the ground.

Seed drill

Now the field is ready for seeds to be planted in it. This tractor is pulling a seed drill which does that job.

Seeds are held in this box. It is called a hopper.

The drill makes grooves in the earth. Seeds drop down into them.

These spikes cover the planted seeds with earth.

Spreaders and sprayers

Crops need food called fertilizer to grow well. They may need protection from insects and diseases, too. The machines on this page spread fertilizer over fields or spray them with pest-killing chemicals.

Manure spreader

Farm animals produce a lot of waste. It is called manure or dung. It is a very good fertilizer.

A tractor pulls this machine to spread manure over crops. It is called a manure spreader.

This tool is called a grab (see page 14). It fills the spreader with manure.

As the tractor moves, its P.T.O. (Power Take-Off) pulls four chains along the floor of the spreader.

Chains carry the manure to the back of the machine.

These spiked wheels chop up the manure. They are called shredders.

The shredders spread a layer of chopped manure onto the field by flinging it out of the back of the spreader.

Sprayer

Some farmers spray fields with chemicals called pesticides to kill insects and diseases. They are poisonous, so farmers must use them very carefully.

The machine attached to this tractor is called a sprayer. As the tractor moves, it sprays out exactly the right amount of pesticide.

Super sprayers

In some countries, fields are huge. Farmers attach very wide sprayers behind their tractors to spray their land as quickly as possible. This sprayer is about as long as two buses.

This is an extra tank of pesticide.

Farmers do not spray pesticides on windy days. The chemicals must not blow around.

This is called the boom. It is the main part of the spraying machine.

This tank holds the pesticide mixed with some water.

The mixture is pumped through these pipes.

A pump pushes pesticide out of these tiny holes, called nozzles.

This boom has more than 20 nozzles.

Combine harvester

This farming machine is called a combine harvester. It combines two jobs in one machine. First, it cuts and gathers up crops such as wheat, peas and barley. This is called harvesting. Then it separates grains from their stalks. This is called threshing. Here you can see how it works.

Sorting out

Many crops are stalks with grains at the top. A combine cuts and pulls in the whole stalk.

Inside the cab

Some combine harvesters have computers in the cab. They tell the driver how full the grain tank is and how well the machine is working.

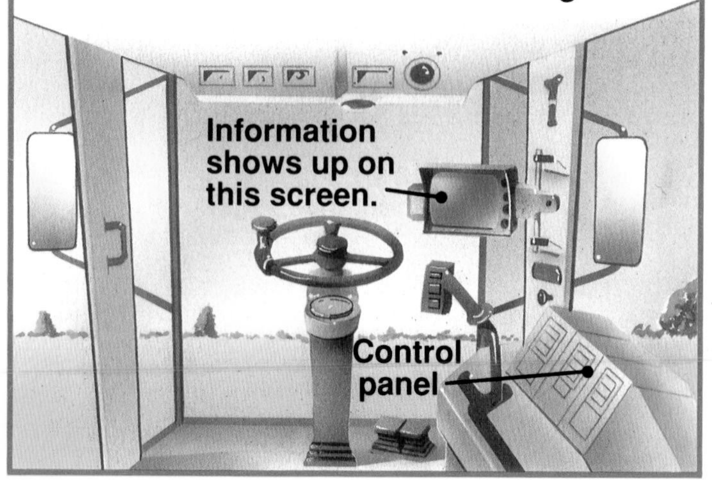

Metal teeth at the front of the combine push through the field. They divide it into strips.

A blade cuts the stalks off at the bottom. It makes about 1,000 cuts a minute.

This wheel, called a reel, spins around. It is covered with metal spikes called tines.

The tines push the cut stalks into the combine harvester.

Inside the machine, a stone trap catches any stones.

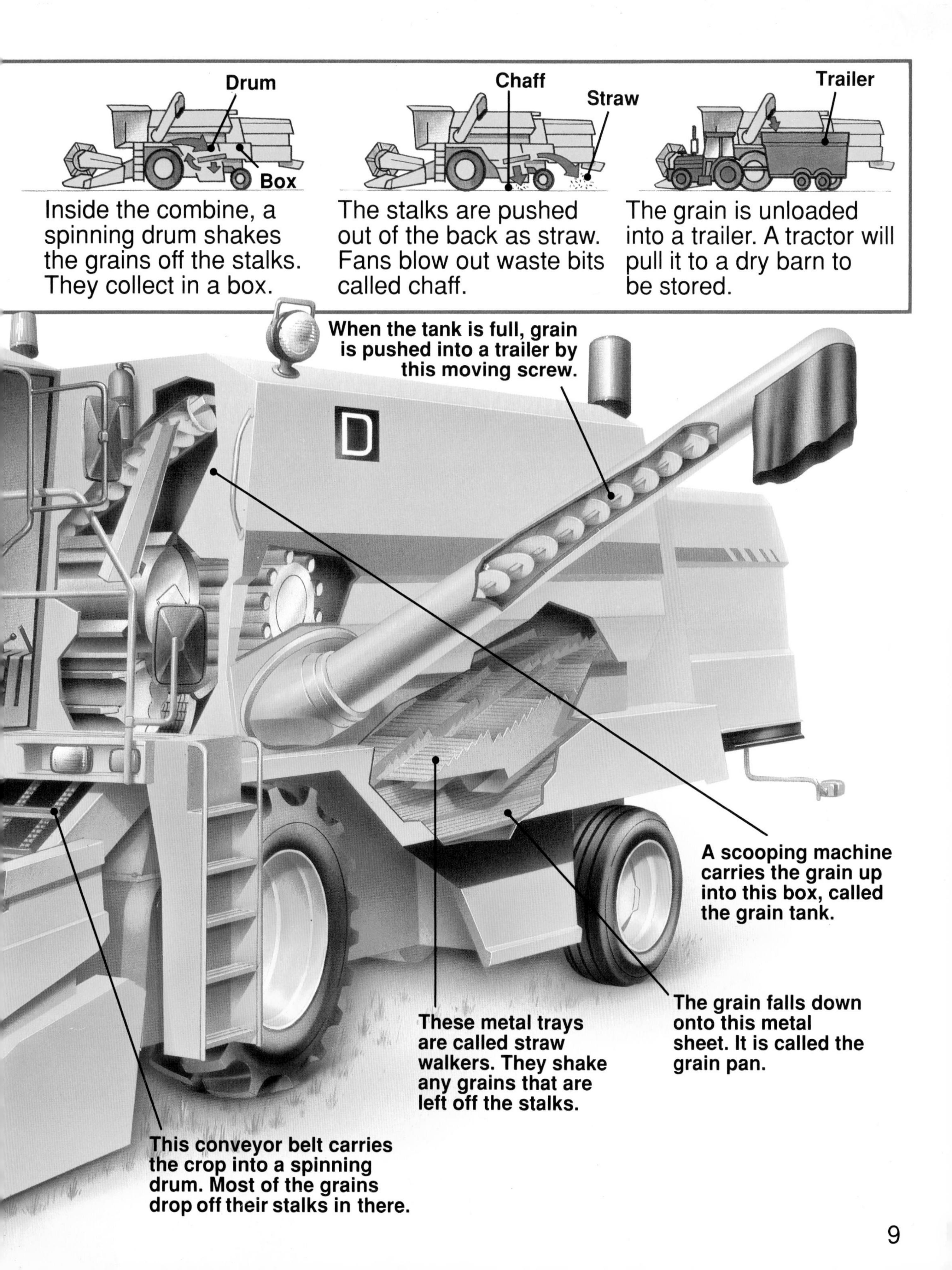
Drum
Box
Inside the combine, a spinning drum shakes the grains off the stalks. They collect in a box.
Chaff
Straw
The stalks are pushed out of the back as straw. Fans blow out waste bits called chaff.
Trailer
The grain is unloaded into a trailer. A tractor will pull it to a dry barn to be stored.
D
When the tank is full, grain is pushed into a trailer by this moving screw.
A scooping machine carries the grain up into this box, called the grain tank.
The grain falls down onto this metal sheet. It is called the grain pan.
These metal trays are called straw walkers. They shake any grains that are left off the stalks.
This conveyor belt carries the crop into a spinning drum. Most of the grains drop off their stalks in there.

Hay and straw

Farmers use these machines to cut and gather hay and straw. Straw is used as bedding for farm animals. Hay is dried grass, which they eat.

Mower

This tractor is pulling a grass mower. The mower cuts grass and leaves it in rows called swaths on the field.

These blades spin around about 3,000 times in a minute. They cut the grass.

Power from the tractor's P.T.O. goes through this metal arm to make the blades turn.

Swath

Swath turner

Straw and grass must be completely dry before they are made into bundles called bales. This tool is called a swath turner. It helps dry swaths out by turning them over.

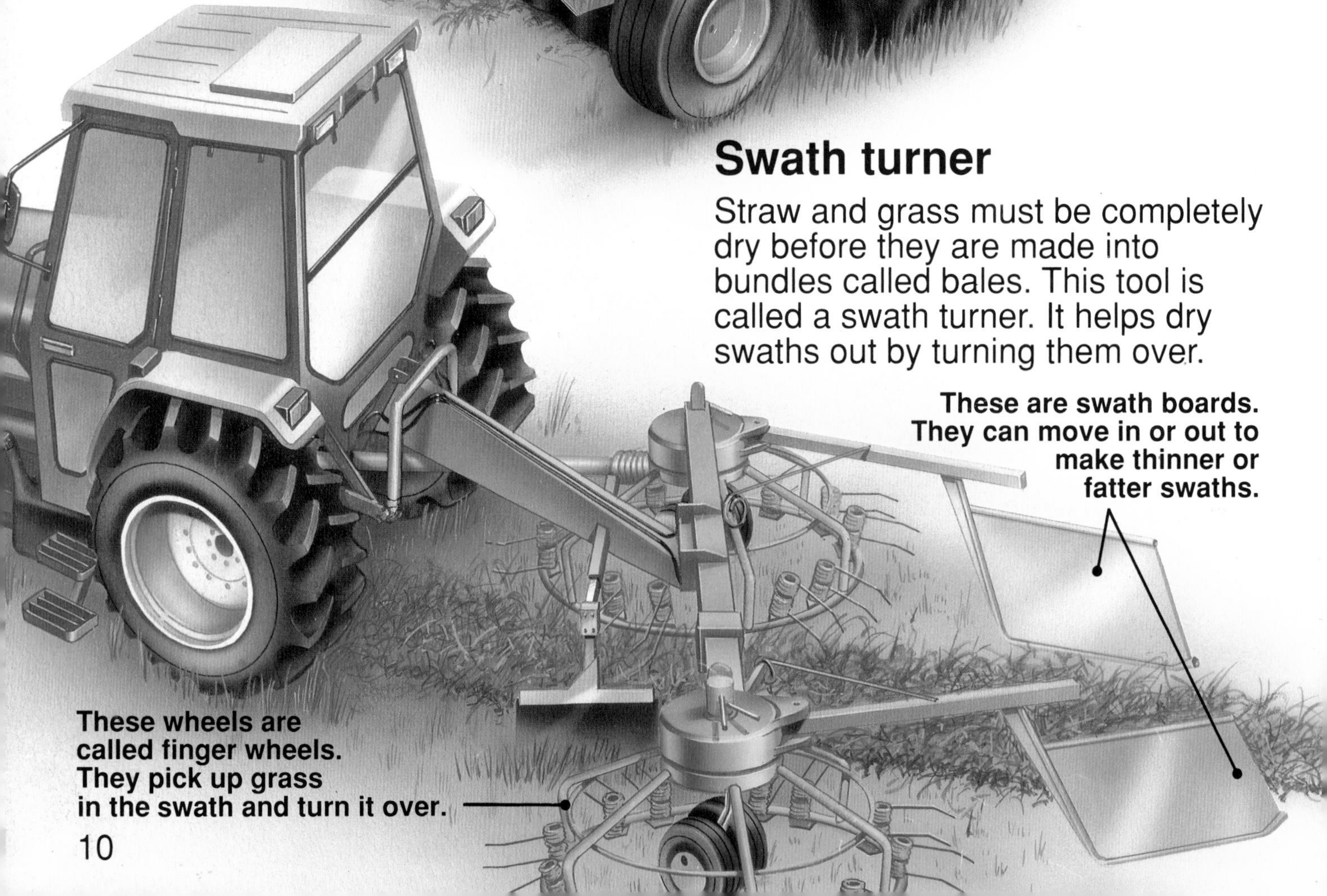

These are swath boards. They can move in or out to make thinner or fatter swaths.

These wheels are called finger wheels. They pick up grass in the swath and turn it over.

Baler

Wrapping hay and straw into bales makes it easier to carry them around. This machine makes round bales. It is called a round baler.

How it works

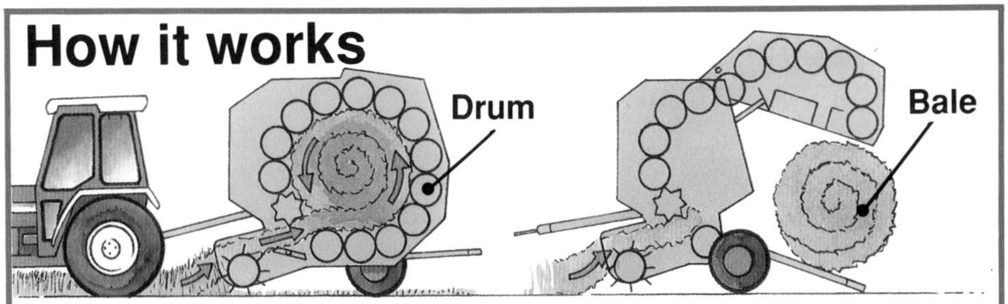

Drum

Bale

Metal fingers at the front of the baler push hay and straw into the machine. Spinning drums roll them into a ball.

String ties the bale up tight. Then the top half of the baler opens. The new bale falls out of the back onto the field.

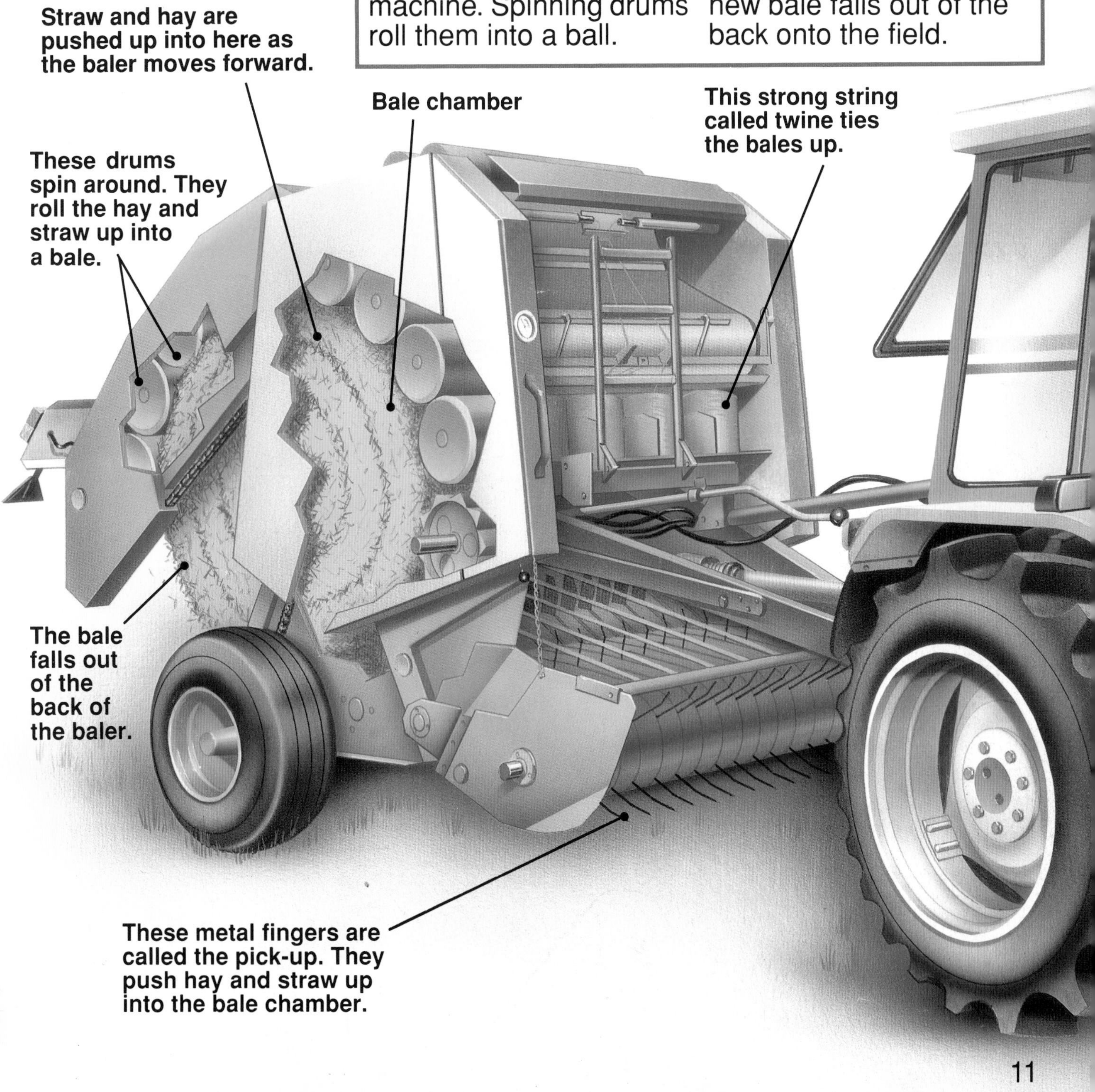

Straw and hay are pushed up into here as the baler moves forward.

Bale chamber

This strong string called twine ties the bales up.

These drums spin around. They roll the hay and straw up into a bale.

The bale falls out of the back of the baler.

These metal fingers are called the pick-up. They push hay and straw up into the bale chamber.

Feeding animals

In the summer, animals can eat grass or crops grown for them. This sort of animal food is called forage. Farmers harvest forage crops in the summer and make them into a food called silage. They can feed this to their animals in winter, when less forage grows.

Forage to silage

The forage harvester picks up cut grass. It chops it up and blows it into a trailer.

The chopped-up forage is tipped into a metal box called a dumpbox back in the farmyard.

A blower blows forage into a tower called a silo. Inside here, it slowly becomes silage.

Forage harvester

This machine is a forage harvester. It picks up forage crops and chops them up as it moves.

This is the pick-up. It spins around very fast, picking up forage with metal spikes called tines.

The spinning cutterhead is like a fast fan. It blows the forage up this spout into the trailer.

This is the cutterhead. It has 15 steel knives, which chop forage as the cutterhead whizzes around.

Dumpbox and blower

At one end of the dumpbox, a blower blows forage into the tower silo with a powerful fan. Inside the silo, forage pickles as if it was in vinegar. This turns it into silage.

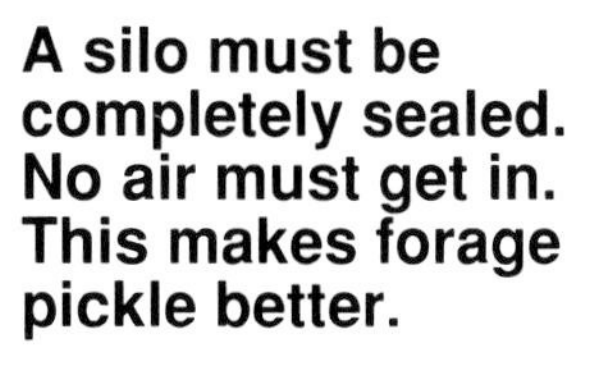

A silo must be completely sealed. No air must get in. This makes forage pickle better.

The silo is sealed shut all summer while the forage becomes silage.

It is dangerous to go into a silo. Silage gives off smelly gases so there is no air inside for humans to breathe.

A moving metal belt carries the forage up to the other end of the dumpbox.

These toothed wheels turn around. They push the forage towards the blower.

This is the blower. It needs power from a tractor's P.T.O. to make it work.

The forage is blown very fast up this pipe.

It takes about 45 minutes to blow all the silage out of the dumpbox into the silo.

Lifters

Tools can be attached to the front and back of tractors. These tools are specially built to lift and carry around the farm.

Grab

This tool is called a grab. The farmer can fasten it to his tractor to pick up and move silage or manure.

This is the grab.

The tractor driver controls the grab with levers inside the cab.

These extra tines stop anything from falling out of the side of the grab.

These prongs are called tines. They are arranged like rows of teeth.

How the grab works

Tines

When the grab is near the manure, the driver pulls a lever. Its tines open up like a mouth.

Another lever makes the tines close around some manure. The grab lifts up with its load.

The tines open to let the manure fall out where the driver wants to unload it.

Bale fork

Bales of hay and straw are heavy and difficult to lift. Farmers fasten a tool called a bale fork to their tractor to move them around the farm.

This spike sticks deep into the bale.

This metal pedal pushes the bale off the spikes.

This smaller spike stops the bale swaying from side to side as the tractor drives along.

How it works

As the tractor moves forward, the fork sticks into the bale.

The bale fork lifts up to carry loads, so that the farmer can see the road.

The tractor lowers the bale fork. A pedal pushes the bale off.

Fork-lift tractor

Farmers need to move sacks of grain, cattle food or fertilizer around the farm. They can fasten a fork-lift to the front of a tractor to do this.

Boom

These two prongs are called forks. They are on the end of a metal arm called a boom. Together, they make the fork-lift.

Sacks rest on wooden trays laid on top of the forks.

Root crop machines

Farmers use these machines to plant and harvest vegetables such as potatoes and carrots. We eat their roots, so they are called root crops.

Potato planter

This is an automatic potato planter. It plants small potatoes, called seed potatoes, under the ground as it moves.

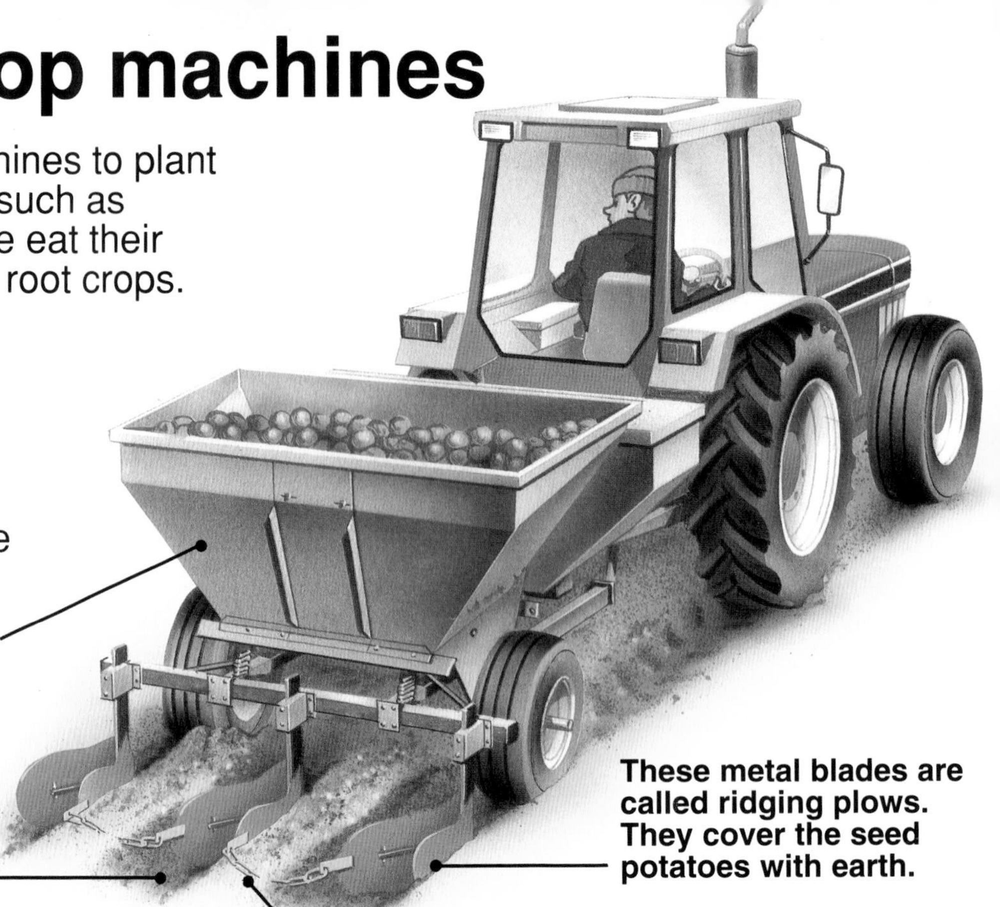

This box is called the hopper. It can hold 30 sacks of seed potatoes.

The seed potatoes fall into grooves called furrows in the field.

These metal blades are called ridging plows. They cover the seed potatoes with earth.

Chains drag over the earth to make nicely shaped ridges.

Root crop harvester

This is a root crop harvester. It is harvesting potatoes.

The tractor guides the harvester between the rows of potato plants.

Blades called shares slice under the potatoes. They lift the whole plant out of the ground.

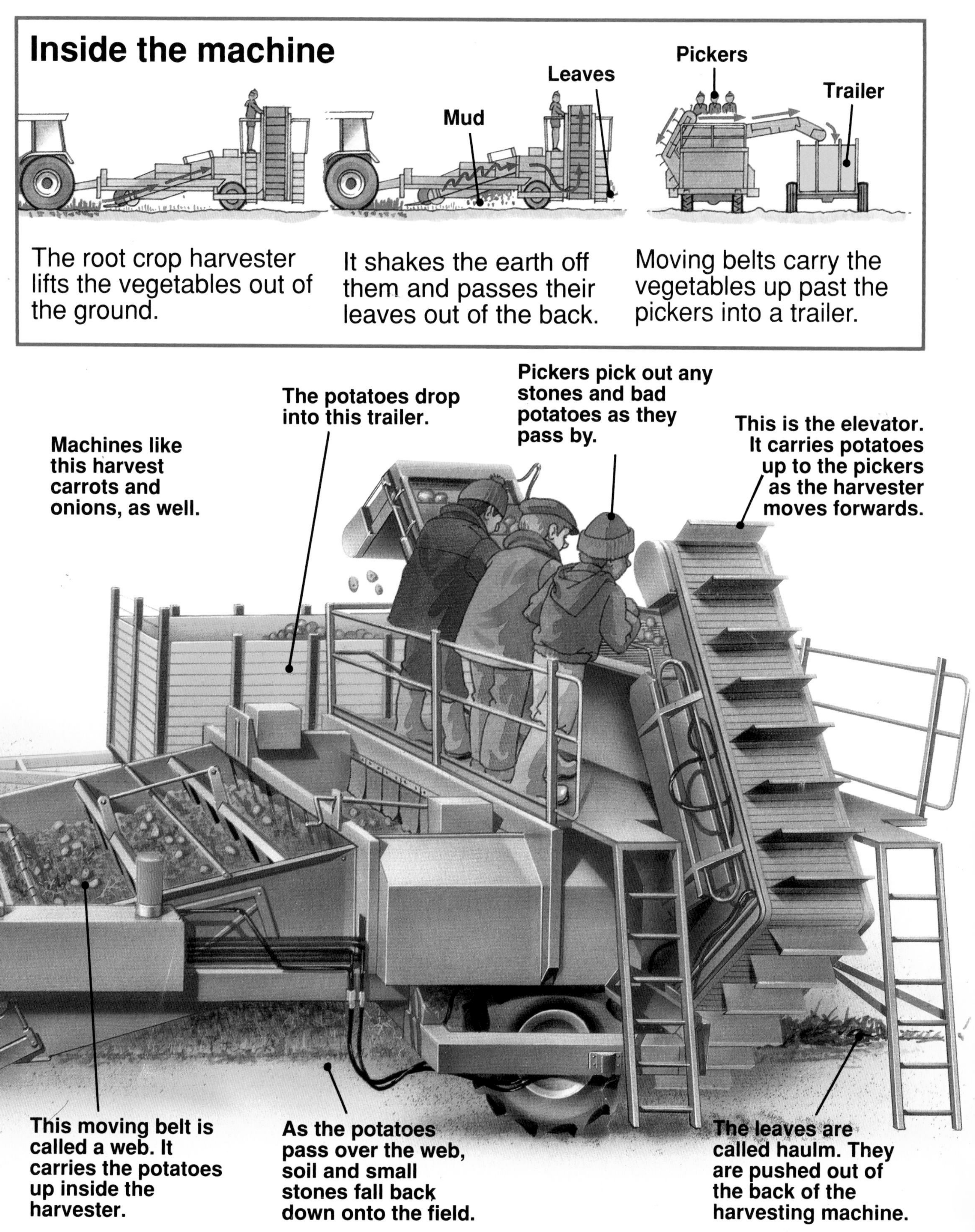
Inside the machine
Leaves
Mud
Pickers
Trailer
The root crop harvester lifts the vegetables out of the ground.
It shakes the earth off them and passes their leaves out of the back.
Moving belts carry the vegetables up past the pickers into a trailer.
The potatoes drop into this trailer.
Pickers pick out any stones and bad potatoes as they pass by.
This is the elevator. It carries potatoes up to the pickers as the harvester moves forwards.
Machines like this harvest carrots and onions, as well.
This moving belt is called a web. It carries the potatoes up inside the harvester.
As the potatoes pass over the web, soil and small stones fall back down onto the field.
The leaves are called haulm. They are pushed out of the back of the harvesting machine.

Giant tractor

Ordinary tractors are not powerful enough for some farming jobs. Huge machines like this do them. This tractor usually works in the big wheat fields of North America. It can work for a long time without stopping.

Wheels and weight

Tractors like this are very heavy. They need eight wheels to carry their enormous weight.

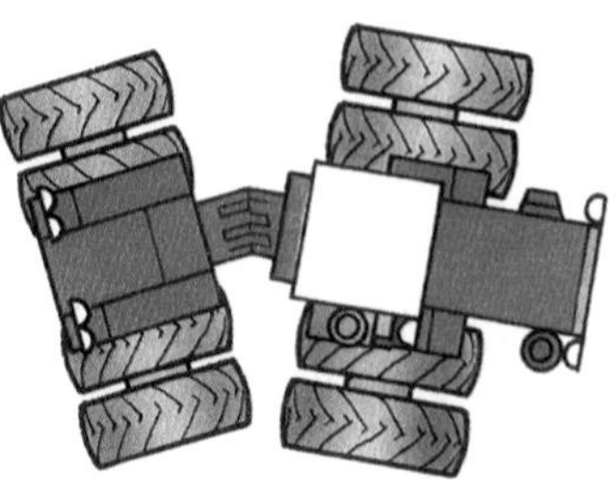

All eight tires turn together to make the huge tractor move and turn around.

The tractor's tires are very wide. This helps them grip more ground to pull the tractor along.

Giant tractors like this are heavy and slow. They can only go about as fast as a bicycle.

This tractor can pull heavy loads and other farming tools behind it, too.

Headlights

Big Bud

This is one of the biggest tractors in the world. It is called Big Bud. Its tires are taller than a man.

Big Bud was specially built to work on big farms in North America.

These eight wide tires spread the tractor's weight out over more ground. They help stop it from sinking into the field.

This tractor can work for about 24 hours without needing more fuel.

This is the air filter. It stops dust from getting into the engine and damaging it.

Sitting in this cab is like looking out of an upstairs window of a house.

The driver can listen to the radio or cassettes while he works long hours.

Giant tractors often work at night, too. They have lights at the front and at the back.

This thick glass stops too much engine noise from getting into the cab.

Some of the wheat fields in North America are so long that it can take an hour to drive from one end to the other.

This tractor's engine is much more powerful than an ordinary tractor's engine.

Loaders

These machines are built to pick up loads. They are called loaders. Three different types of loaders work on farms.

Tractor loader

This is a tractor loader. It has a bucket used for scooping things into attached in front of its cab.

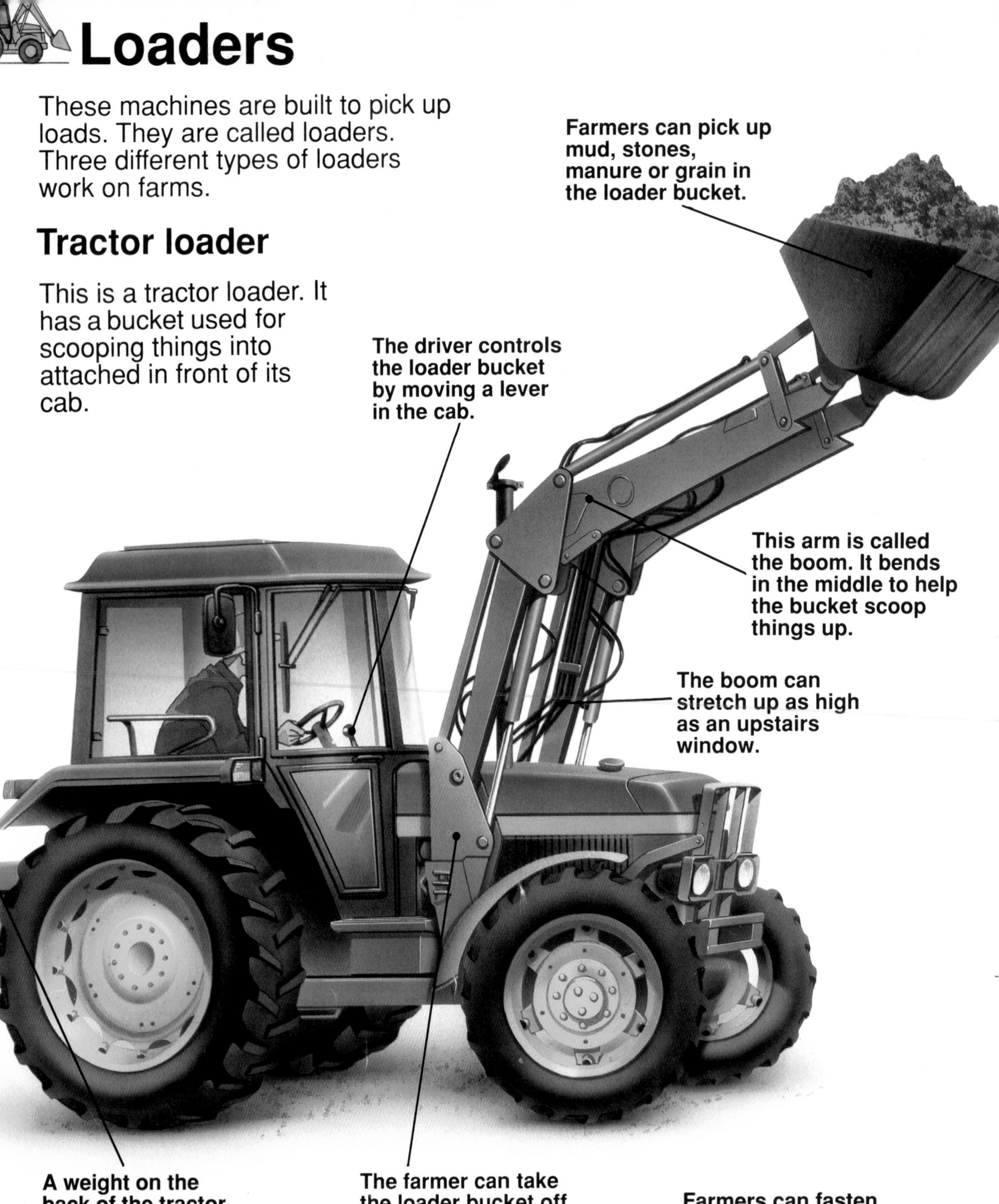

A weight on the back of the tractor stops it falling forward when it carries heavy loads. It is called the counterweight.

The farmer can take the loader bucket off the tractor in only a few minutes.

Farmers can fasten other tools to the front of loaders. You can see some on pages 14 and 15.

Skid-steer loader

This skid-steer loader does smaller loading jobs. It is called a skid-steer loader because it can turn around so quickly and easily it is like skidding.

Telescopic loader

Loaders like this are called telescopic loaders. On these machines, the lifting arm slides out from inside a straight metal case, just like a telescope does.

The driver sits in this small cab.

Metal bars called rollbars protect him in case the loader topples over.

Skid-steer loaders can stop and spin around to face the other way in a very small space.

The driver controls the loader with foot pedals in the cab.

Lift and load

A skid-steer loader can scoop things up when its bucket tilts like this.

Its boom can reach up and unload things high above the cab.

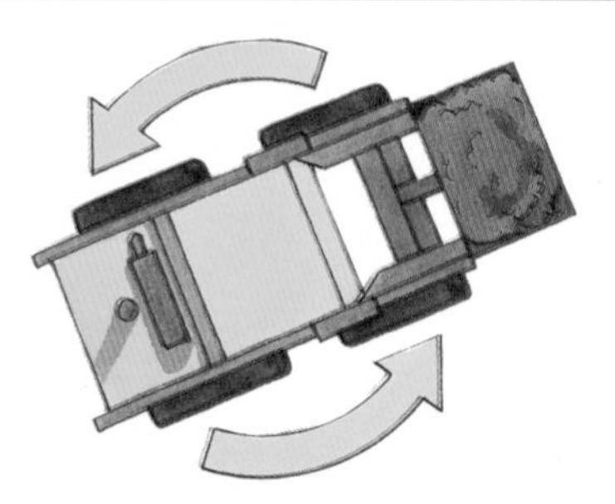

The farmer can steer the loader so that it turns around in a circle.

Tractors do many unusual jobs on a farm. Here, they have tools fastened to them for digging ditches, cutting hedges and banging in fence posts.

Ditch digger

If a field stays too wet after rain, crops cannot grow in it. The farmer must get the water off the field, or drain it.

This tractor is using a tool called a backhoe to dig drainage ditches. The water will flow off the field and into the ditches.

Hedge-trimmer

Farmers have to keep hedges tidy. This tractor has an arm called a hedge-trimmer fixed to it. As the tractor moves, the trimmer's metal blades cut the tops off hedges.

The backhoe has its own seat. It faces backwards so the farmer can see where he is digging.

These are the controls for the bucket.

The digging arm can move up and down or from side to side.

The backhoe's bucket has metal teeth along its edge. They can cut through hard earth.

Metal legs stop the tractor from toppling over backward as it digs.

This frame fastens the backhoe and its seat to the back of the tractor.

Post driver

Tractors can help the farmer put fences around his fields. This tractor has a tool called a post driver attached to it. It pushes fence posts into the ground. The farmer joins them up with wire.

This metal frame fastens the post driver to the back of the tractor. It is very strong.

This heavy weight is like a hammer. It bangs the posts into the ground.

Some frames can swing around to work on either side of the tractor.

This post driver can bash in a post every 40 seconds.

Post

These metal legs are called stabilizers. They hold the tractor steady as it thumps in posts.

Post drivers are sometimes called post bashers.

Pushing power

Post

The farmer slides a wooden post into a slot in the post driver.

He puts the post driver above the place where he wants a fence post.

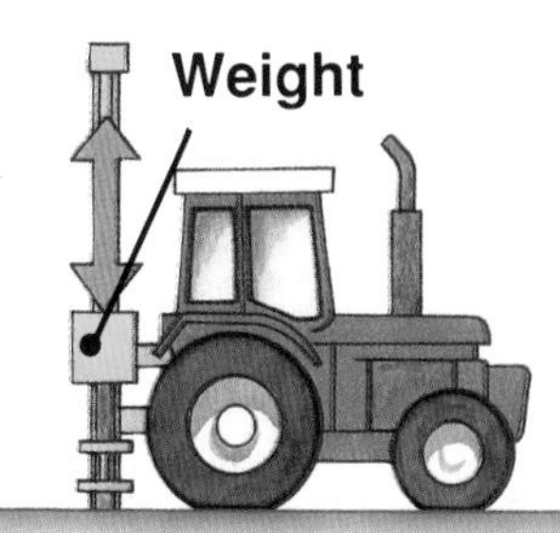

Heavy weights slide down the driver and bang the post into the ground.

Crawler tractor

This tractor has rubber tracks instead of tires. They are called crawler tracks. Farmers use crawler tractors like this in wet, muddy fields where ordinary tractors might get stuck. They can also pull heavy loads and farming tools without their tracks slipping or sinking.

Inside the cab

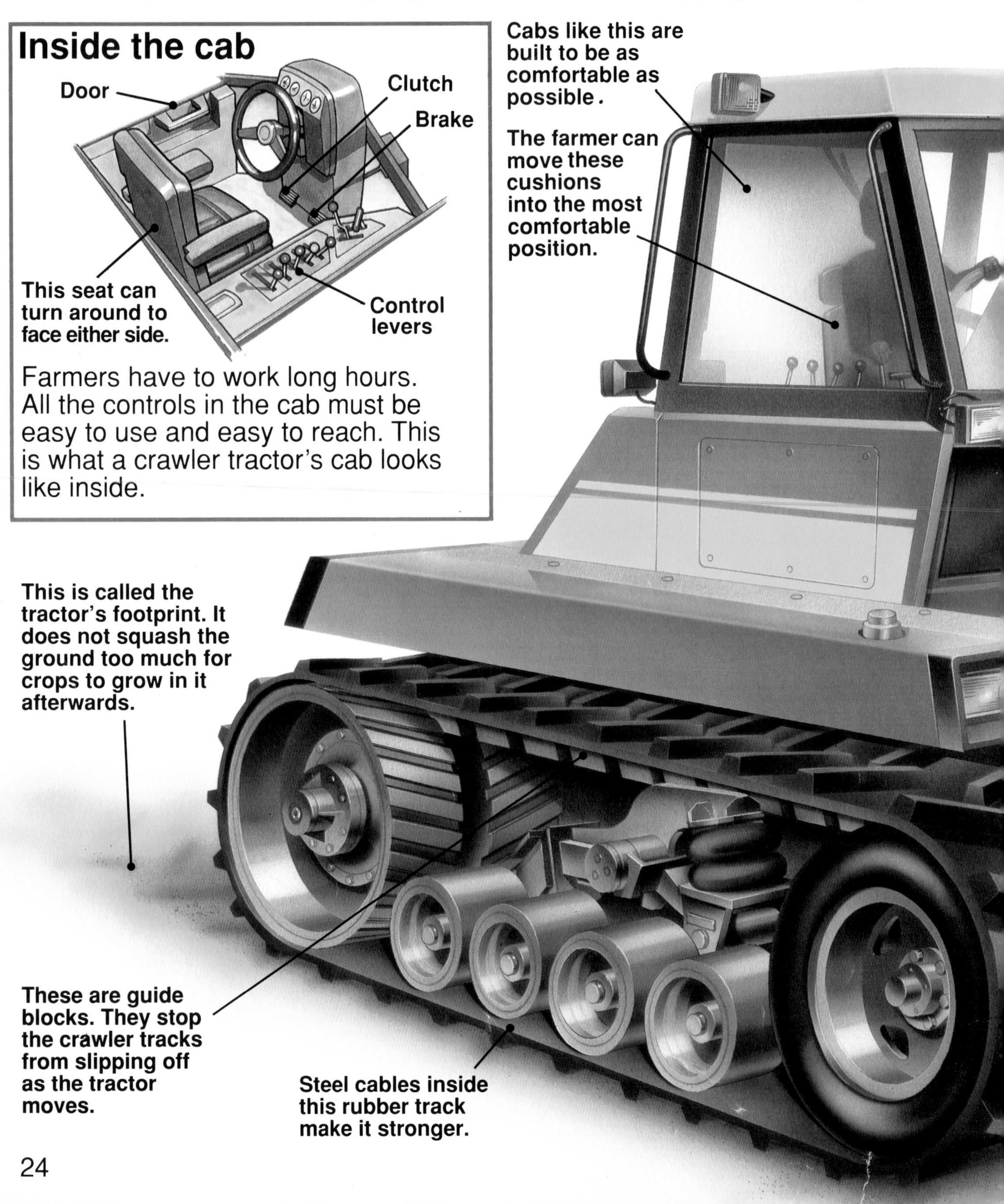

Farmers have to work long hours. All the controls in the cab must be easy to use and easy to reach. This is what a crawler tractor's cab looks like inside.

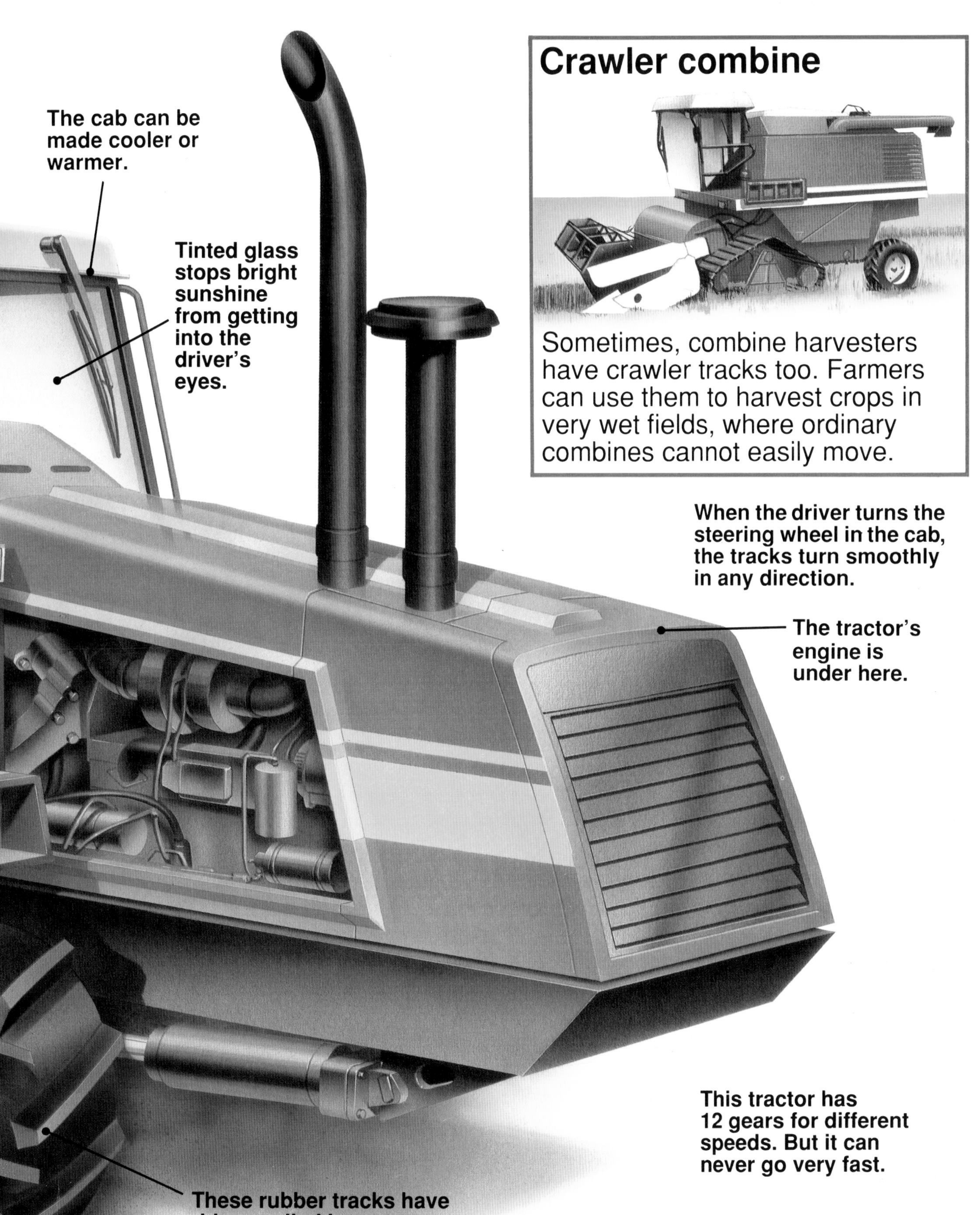

Crawler combine

Sometimes, combine harvesters have crawler tracks too. Farmers can use them to harvest crops in very wet fields, where ordinary combines cannot easily move.

Fruit-farming machines

Farmers who grow fruit need different sorts of farming machines. You can see two of them here.

Berry harvester

Fruit can easily be damaged when it is picked. Then it is not worth as much money.

This machine harvests grapes and berries without squashing them.

Looking inside

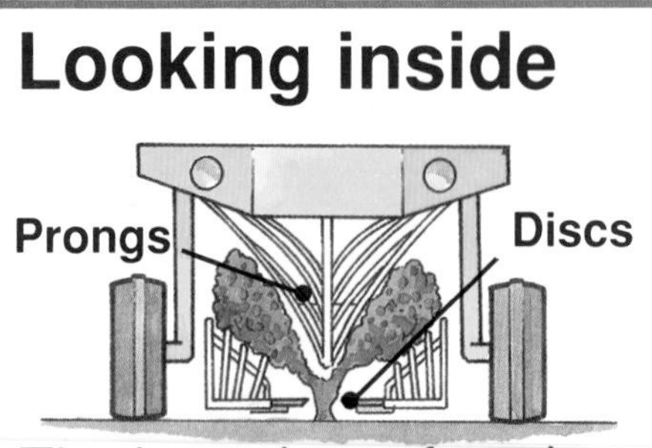

The branches of each bush are pushed into two halves by metal prongs and plastic discs.

Plastic fingers above the discs gently tap each bush. Berries drop off into trays.

The trays slowly move, carrying the berries up to pickers. They pack the fruit into boxes.

The driver drives the machine very slowly over the bushes.

These metal prongs part the bush into two, like hair.

The bushes push these flexible discs back as they go into the machine.

These plastic fingers knock the berries off.

The berries are slowly carried up here on a moving belt.

The picker fills plastic boxes with berries. When one is full, he stacks it up while the other picker fills a box.

The leaves and dirt fall out of the bottom of the machine.

Mistblower

This is a mistblower. It is specially built to spray tall fruit trees and grape vines with chemicals that kill insects and diseases.

Trees and vines are too tall for ordinary sprayers, like the one on page 7, to reach them.

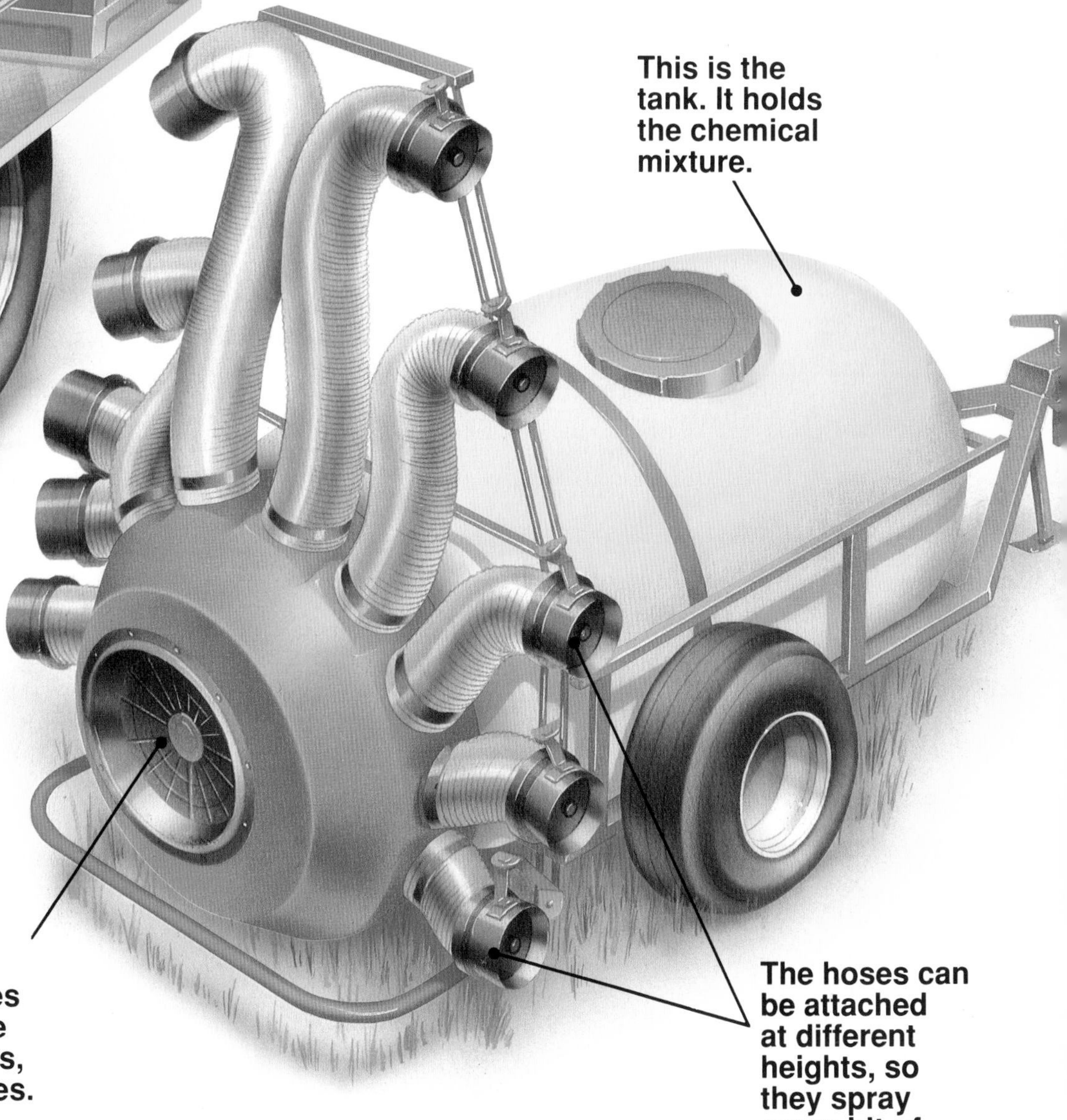

This is the tank. It holds the chemical mixture.

This fan behind the tank pushes the mixture out of pipes, called hoses.

The hoses can be attached at different heights, so they spray every bit of the plant.

Special tractors

Farmers need different tractors for different jobs. The ones on this page are built to do special sorts of work.

Three-wheeler

This tractor has three huge wheels. They hold so much air that the tractor does not squash the soil.

Its job is to spread fertilizer over big fields just before seeds are planted in them.

This light flashes when the tractor is moving on roads.

This tractor's cab is much higher above the ground than on ordinary tractors.

This trailer is full of fertilizer.

These big, round tires spread the tractor's weight over the field.

The engine is under the cab, not in front of it. This means that all three wheels help spread out its weight.

Mini-tractor

This tractor is too small for farm-work. People use mini-tractors like this to mow the grass on golf-courses, in parks or in large gardens.

Narrow tractor

Tractors like this can work between rows of grapevines or fruit trees. They are very narrow, so that they don't damage any crops.

A.T.V.

Some farmers ride around their fields on bikes like these. They are called A.T.V.s. This is short for All-Terrain Vehicle, which means they can go over any sort of ground.

Tractors old and new

Farming has changed a lot in the last 100 years. Tractors and other farming machines make the farmer's job much easier than it used to be.

On these two pages you can see some of the first tractors, as well as some of the newest farm machines that work in the fields today.

Early tractor

This tractor was built in Canada around 80 years ago. At that time, more and more farmers started using machines to do their farm-work.

This tractor uses a fuel called kerosene to make it work.

These wheels are made of solid metal. They have ridges cut into them to help them to grip, though.

Three wheeler

This tractor was built in 1914. It only has three wheels. It was popular because it was tough and cheap to run.

This type of tractor can use gas in its engine.

This tractor is called 'The Bull'.

Lighter tractor

By the 1930s, many tractors looked like this. They have rubber tires. These are lighter than metal ones are which makes tractors easier to drive.

Rubber tires grip the ground better than metal wheels.

Systems tractor

This machine works on many farms in Europe today. It is called a systems tractor. Farmers fasten tools to the front, middle and back of it, so it can do three jobs at once.

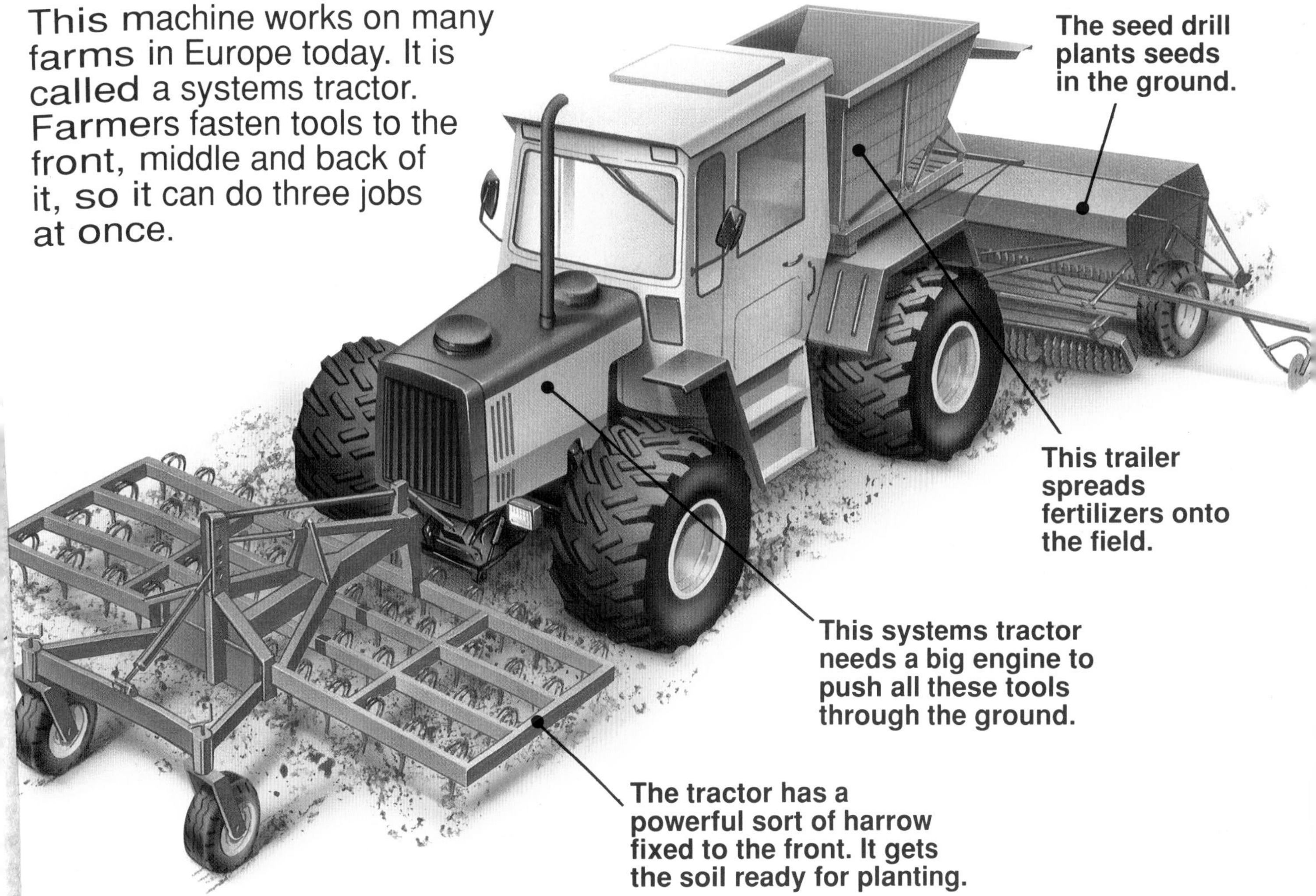

The seed drill plants seeds in the ground.

This trailer spreads fertilizers onto the field.

This systems tractor needs a big engine to push all these tools through the ground.

The tractor has a powerful sort of harrow fixed to the front. It gets the soil ready for planting.

Gantry

This wide machine is called a gantry. It farms big fields without squashing the soil by making too many trips up and down it.

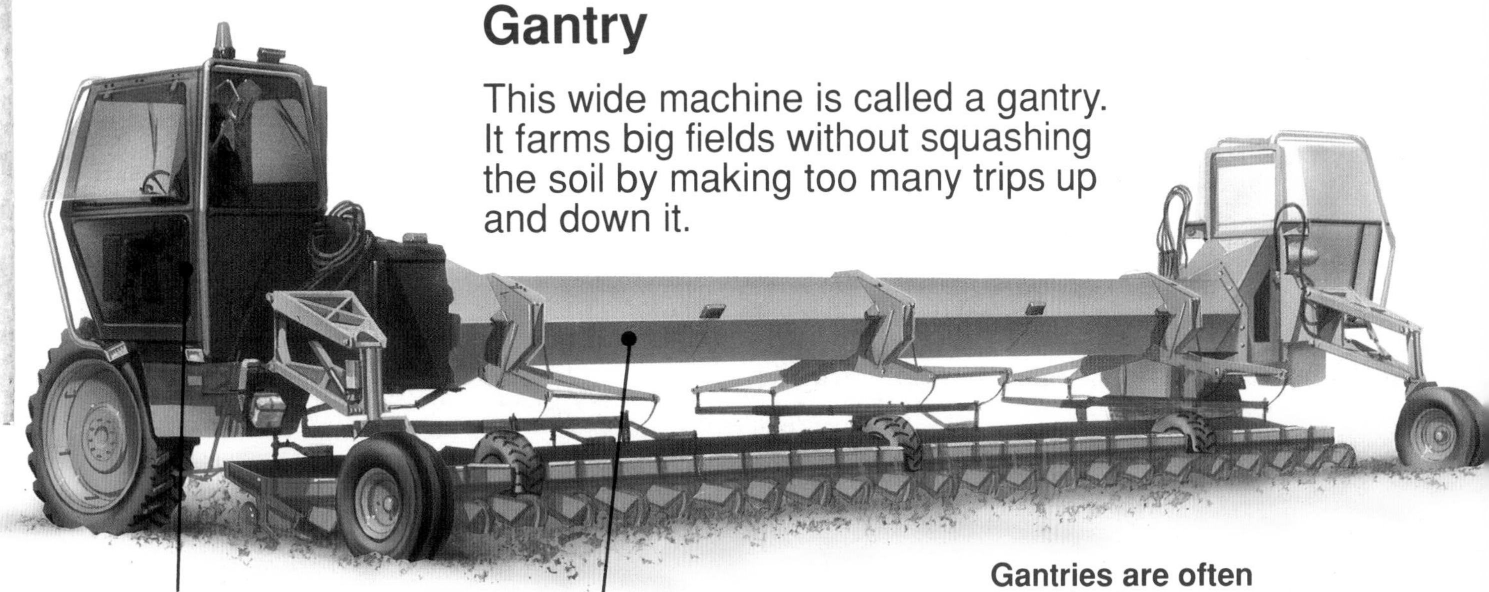

The driver sits in this cab. He has a clear view of the field and the gantry as he drives.

Some gantries are as long as six men lying down head to toe.

Gantries are often used by farmers who grow flowers. This sort of farming is called horticulture.

Index

First published in 1992 by Usborne Publishing Ltd, Usborne House, 83-85 Saffron Hill, London, EC1N 8RT

Printed in Belgium. American edition 1992.

EXPEDITED SHIPMENT

Molly Dugger

From: "Amazon.com Payments" <payments-messages@amazon.com>
To: <orchidsmolly@rica.net>
Cc: <payments-mail@amazon.com>
Sent: Sunday, May 25, 2003 2:21 AM
Subject: Sold -- ship now! Palm Reading: A New Guide to a Mysterious Art by Fairchild, Dennis

Shipping Label

- -

Andrew Leung c/o Amy Woodward
245 Hartford Street
San Francisco, CA 94114

- -

PACKING SLIP:
Amazon Marketplace Item: Palm Reading: A New Guide to a Mysterious Art by Fairchild, Dennis
Listing ID: 0503K920012
SKU:
Quantity: 1

Purchased on: 24-May-2003
Shipped by: orchidsmolly@rica.net
Shipping address:

Ship to: Andrew Leung c/o Amy Woodward
Address Line 1: 245 Hartford Street
Address Line 2:
City: San Francisco
State/Province/Region: CA
Zip/Postal Code: 94114
Country: United States

Buyer Name: Andrew Leung

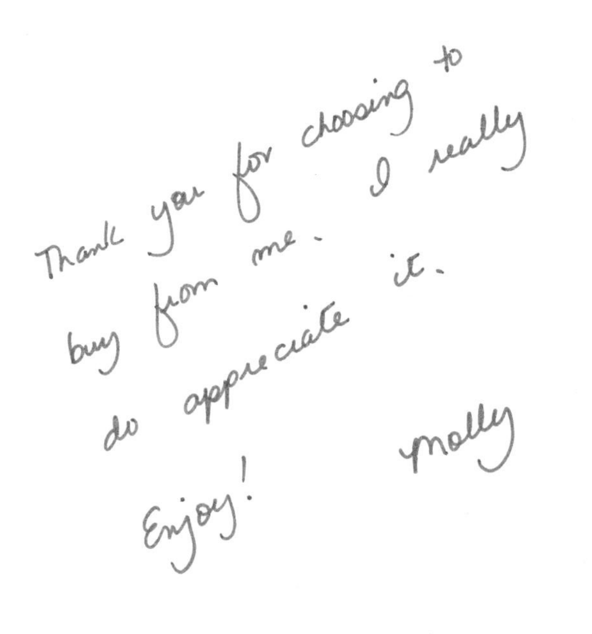

- -

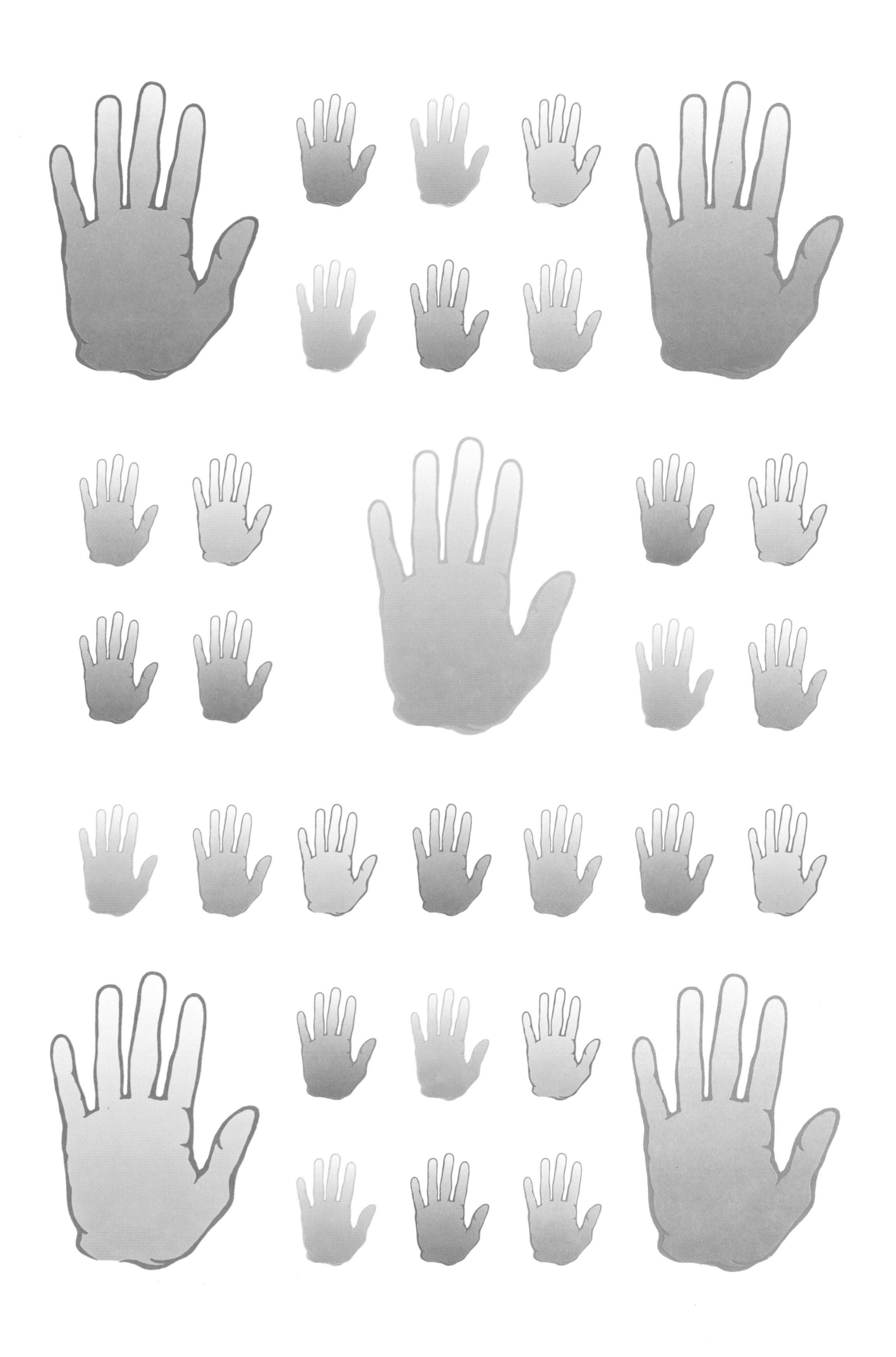

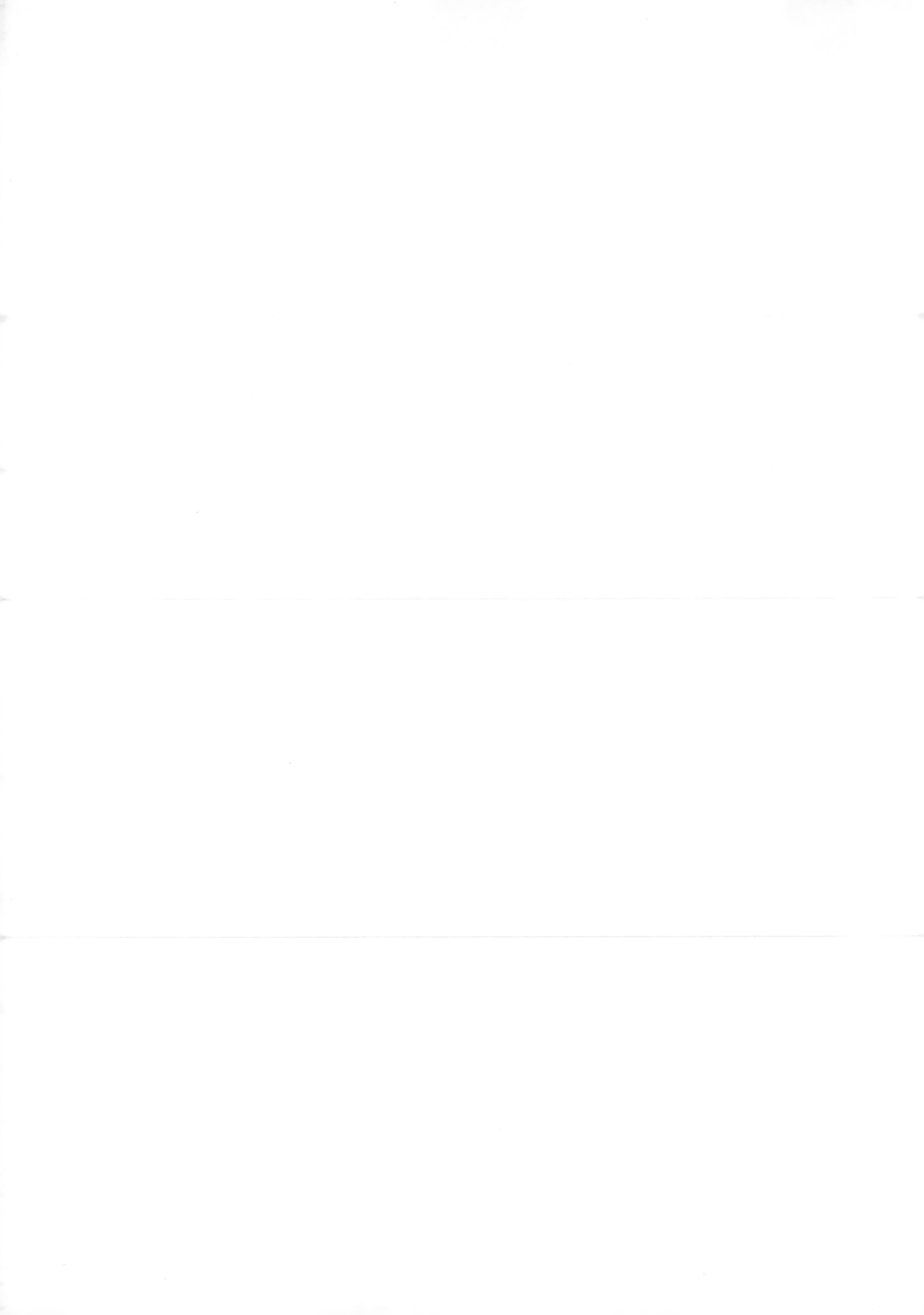

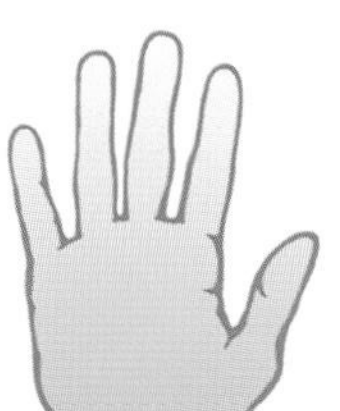

Palm Reading

A New Guide to a Mysterious Art

Written by Dennis Fairchild
Illustrated by Melanie Powell

AN IMPRINT OF RUNNING PRESS
PHILADELPHIA • LONDON

Printed in China

9 8 7 6 5 4 3 2 1
Digit on the right indicates the number of this printing

Library of Congress Cataloging-in-Publication Number
96-67173
ISBN 1-56138-768-1

Cover design by Ken Newbaker
Interior design by Stan Green
Edited by Mary McGuire

Published by Courage Books, an imprint of
Running Press Book Publishers
125 South Twenty-second Street
Philadelphia, Pennsylvania 19103-4399

Contents

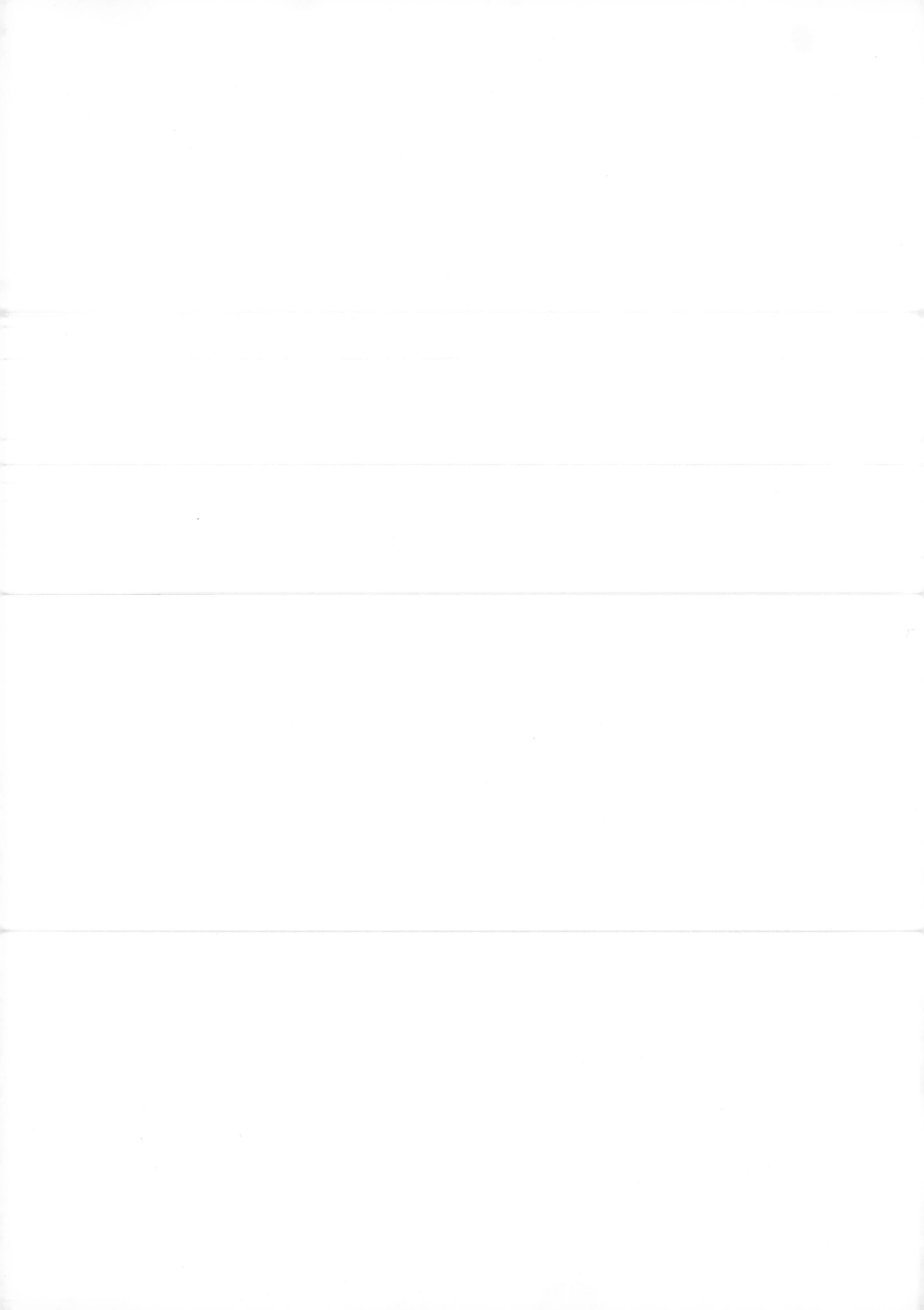

Introduction

Your hands are a miniature map of your personal world—all you need to know is how to read them. Now here's your chance! But first, a little perspective . . .

Palmistry's origins are prehistoric. Back when Aristotle wrote one of the first hand-reading treatises, people were more concerned with surviving monsoons than increasing their self-awareness. Not surprisingly, palmists have been asked to foretell destiny—when will someone marry and have children, will they be successful, and how long will they live?

Most modern palmists do not predict such things as wedding days, the number of children a couple will have, or an untimely end. But what they do read in your hands can give you valuable information about your life and how you interact with the world—information that leads to personal empowerment. Modern palm reading is more in sync with discovering the person who's beneath the skin and uncovering his or her potential. Are you better suited to a people-oriented, high-pressure job or one that's independent, quiet, and contemplative? These are the realms of modern palmistry.

So instead of focusing on future events, you can use palm reading to uncover and illuminate personal traits you can capitalize on and improve. This book updates much of the old-fashioned jargon and presents the art of palm reading in user-friendly terms. Read on, have fun, and remember . . . the future is in your *own* hands.

TIP: One good way to begin identifying hand markings is to photocopy your palms. Then ask your friends, family, and coworkers to photocopy theirs. You'll soon notice that there are many similarites—and differences—among hands. In the chapters that follow you'll learn specific rules for deciphering individual characteristics.

Part I
The Hand

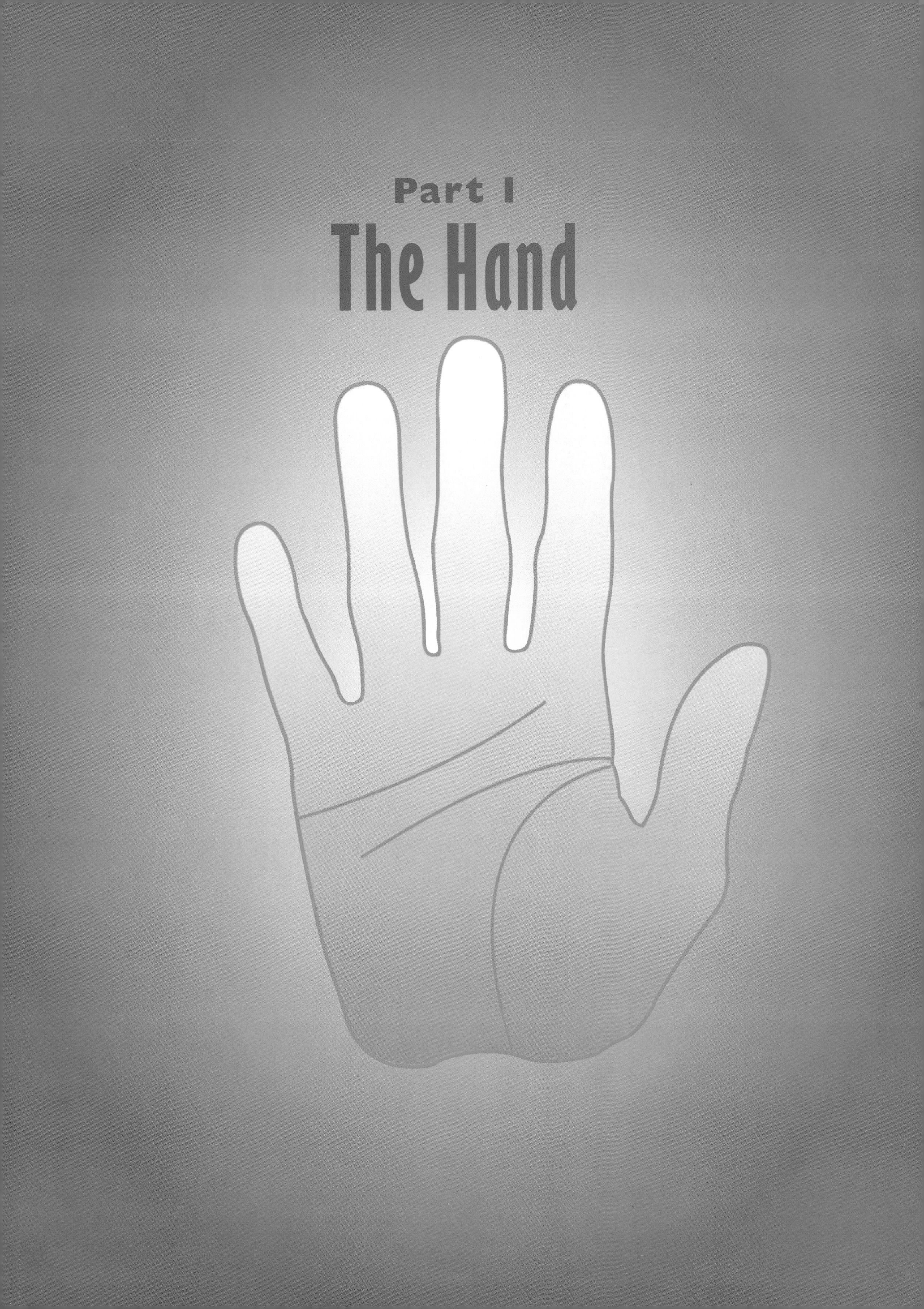

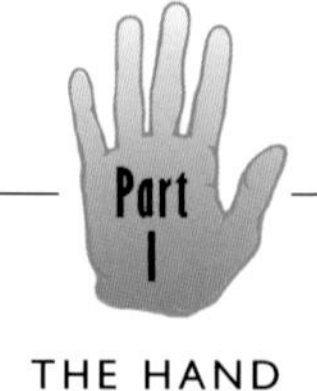

Righties vs. Lefties

Palmists "read" different sets of characteristics in each hand. Your left hand reveals your private side—your fantasies, hopes, and dreams.

More than eighty five percent of the world's people eat, write, and throw baseballs with their right hand. Despite the triumphant achievements of such famous lefties as Leonardo da Vinci, Michelangelo, Benjamin Franklin, Lewis Carroll, and Paul McCartney, ancient notions about the inferiority of lefties persist in our modern, right-handed world. Modern palmistry dismisses these myths but recognizes that left-handed and right-handed individuals have distinct sets of abilities.

Righties

Righties prefer practical, logical reasoning, and tend to be analytical and pragmatic. You always think things through carefully and examine your personal motives before acting. You prefer to play life by the rules and avoid tactics that might be embarrassing. Be careful, though; you may be tempted to relax your efforts when pursuing important personal goals.

Ambitious and hard-working, you invest plenty in your career, and your greatest tests in life are likely to involve some aspect of your work. You support the status quo and are sensitive to what others think of you. Known for your diligence and dependability, you readily assume responsibility and usually do more than your share. Structured, more impersonal and non emotional situations and environments suit you best; you may feel more at home in your office than in your house. Although you desire prestige and status, and you demand respect for your competence, you normally have little interest in publicity (unless you have long index fingers and a deep Head Line).

Lefties

Lefties favor intuitive thinking and tend to be more creative, imaginative, and original. You act often on hunches and have no fear of failure or temporary setbacks, because you know experience can sharpen your abilities. The worst thing you can do is to stop believing that you can realize your goals and objectives.

Scientists say you can endure the pressures of underwater exploration better than righties. (Ever consider scuba diving?) You're more aware of color and sound than righties, too. Many lefties gravitate to the creative, artistic fields.

You're extraordinarily aware of your environment and opinions of others. You have a keen sensitivity to the feelings of others—humans, plants, and animals alike. You can almost feel another's pain yourself, and cannot bear to inflict insult or injury on anyone or anything. Many times you are a bit paranoid and depressive, with a tendency to look at the dark side. Your own sensitivity may scare you or make you feel defensive or vulnerable. Learn to exploit and manage your extra-sensitivity. Be aware of any self-destructive traits you may have and try to change them. Don't focus on damage, disappointment, or failure. Behold a beautiful person doing his or her personal best with the tools at hand.

For the purposes of this book, concentrate on the markings and signs of your right hand, regardless of which hand is dominant. Consider your left hand a reflection of your private, personal self, and your right an indication of how you deal with the outside world. Look at both and note the differences. No one's two hands are the same.

Size

Small

Your hands are considered small if your fingers don't reach past your eyebrows when you rest your wrist on your chin. People with small hands tend to see the big picture but often overlook important details. Self-expression and the bottom line are your major concerns. It's important for you to express yourself in a dramatic, colorful way and to attain recognition. For you, life is a game to be enacted on the stage, and you relish a leading role. Small hands think big!

Because function is as important to you as form, you choose to direct or produce instead of just being a bit player in life. Not given to storybook scenarios, you are more interested in situations that proceed efficiently day to day. You are single-minded, powerfully pursuing your goals with dogged determination. You rely on reason and intellect rather than intuition.

You want desperately to feel needed by a partner and work hard to make yourself indispensable. Most of all, you crave achievement with a steady climb toward status and security. You're also concerned with etiquette, wanting colleagues and lovers to have impeccable manners and to follow "the rules." You have the self-discipline to put aside instant gratification in favor of long-range satisfaction. A word of caution: your pursuit of professional success may lead you to sacrifice intimacy and home life. Constantly review what's personally important to you.

Medium

If your fingers reach your eyebrows when you rest your palm on your chin, you have medium-sized hands. A good mediator, nimble and responsive, you shrug off problems and setbacks easily. You pride yourself on being even-keeled and on not showing prejudice. You're practical, rejecting what is unsuitable, unhealthy, or unnecessary. You enjoy things that make you feel warm and cozy. You seek serenity, comfort, and the good things in life and are willing to do your share.

You're quite generous with those you care about. Nothing makes you happier than caring for loved ones. Still, you can't forget who "owes" you, and who's done you wrong. You have a penchant for detail and are extremely orderly and precise in all you do. You enjoy facts and figures and organizing information, and could use your analytical abilities to great advantage in the fields of accounting, statistics, or computer programming.

Large

Your hands are considered large if, with your wrist resting on your chin, your fingers fall above your eyebrows and almost reach your hairline. Big hands tell of sensitivity, versatility, and curiosity. While small hands skim news headlines, large hands enjoy the small print and cartoons.

Full of mental energy, you are aggressive about getting what you want but flexible enough to see other points of view. You know instinctively how to reach people on their own terms. You enjoy examining and categorizing others, always asking a thousand questions. What upsets you the most is a shortage of answers, dealing with stubbornness from associates, or being told that there is only one way to accomplish a given goal.

A perfectionist, you can be a stickler for exactitude and detail. Perfectionism can also lead to pessimism, since nothing can meet your expectations. Try not to be super-critical of yourself nor of others. In relationships you are cautious and practical. Once you're in a partnership, you tend to find fault with others and complain long and loud about those annoying little habits. No one's perfect. Cut some slack.

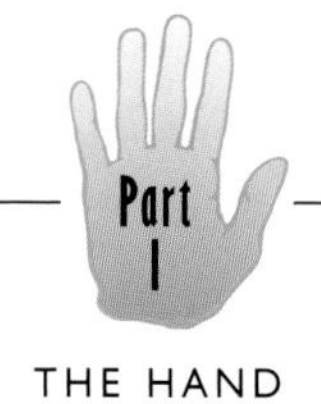

Shape

Most palms are a mix of two primary types. Examine yours closely—one hand shape usually outweighs the other.

Thin Palms

A narrow, upward-pointing rectangular palm—more thin than broad—is the hand of the "feeling" person. You enjoy emotional interchange as well as brainstorming and talking, and have an agile, open mind. You're sensitive, bright, quick, and curious, even though your moods change constantly. Full of mental and touchy-feely energy, you want to know everything about everybody. You tune into emotionalism more than logic. Your emotional state fluctuates noticeably from day to day. In crisis, you try to reason things out to make the most logical choice even if your feelings tell you otherwise. You usually push gut reactions aside in favor of logical constructs, even though your instincts are often right on target.

You love creature comforts and have an innate sense of good taste. You appreciate textures and colors, and feel nurtured by tasty food, nice furnishings, and good sex. Sensual and caring, you want constant companionship but may not be willing to give enough emotional space to a partner. Although faithful and devoted to those you love, you expect total loyalty in return and can be terribly possessive and jealous. Whatever your age, it is unlikely that you've severed the emotional umbilical cord.

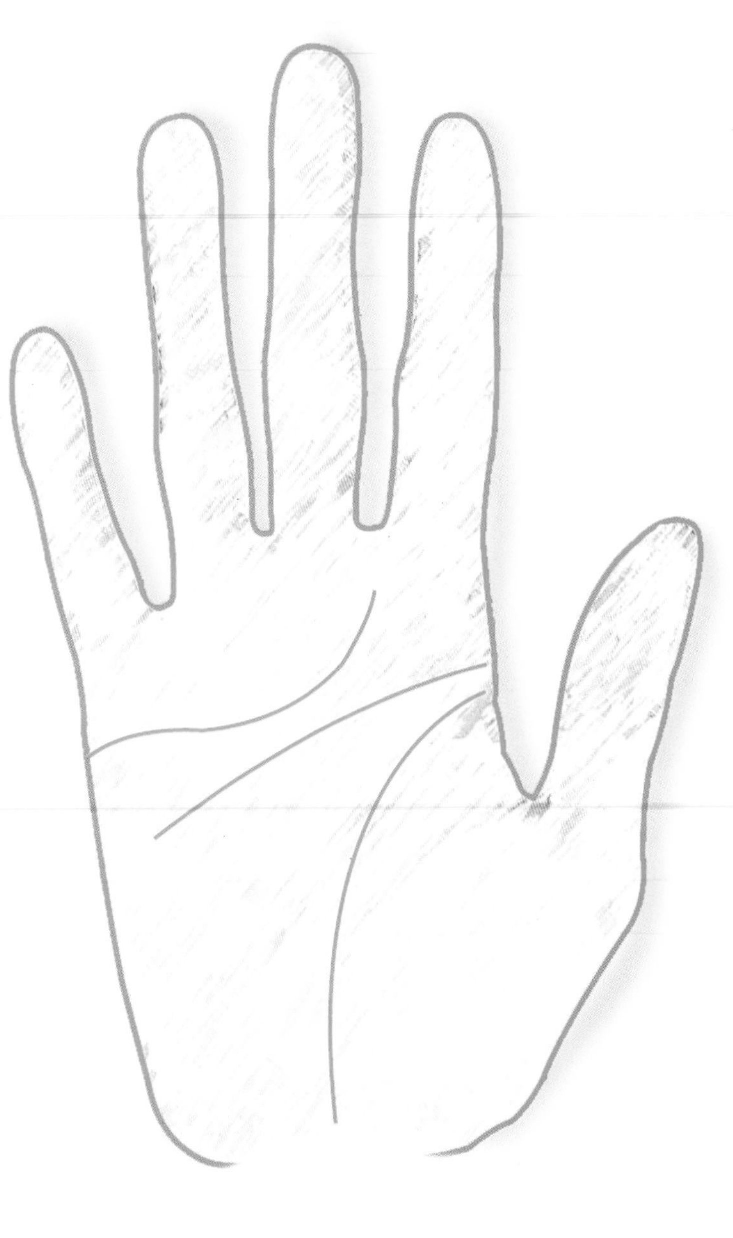

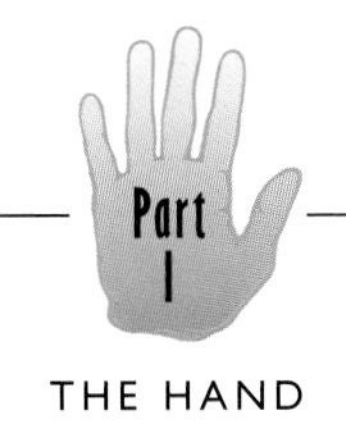

Square Palms

A square palm is known as a "practical" hand. You take nothing for granted and demand that facts be laid out on the table. You possess good reasoning abilities and have a need for security. You shrug off day-to-day upsets and are not easily driven off course. You're a person of action, a hard worker, a doer and achiever. Law and order and no nonsense are your code of honor.

You expect praise for what you do and perform your tasks with such efficiency and modesty that others may not notice. You say what you think but have great difficulty seeing other points of view. You can be extremely critical, but you demand no more from others than you expect from yourself. You have a need to be needed, and you derive emotional satisfaction from being useful and productive.

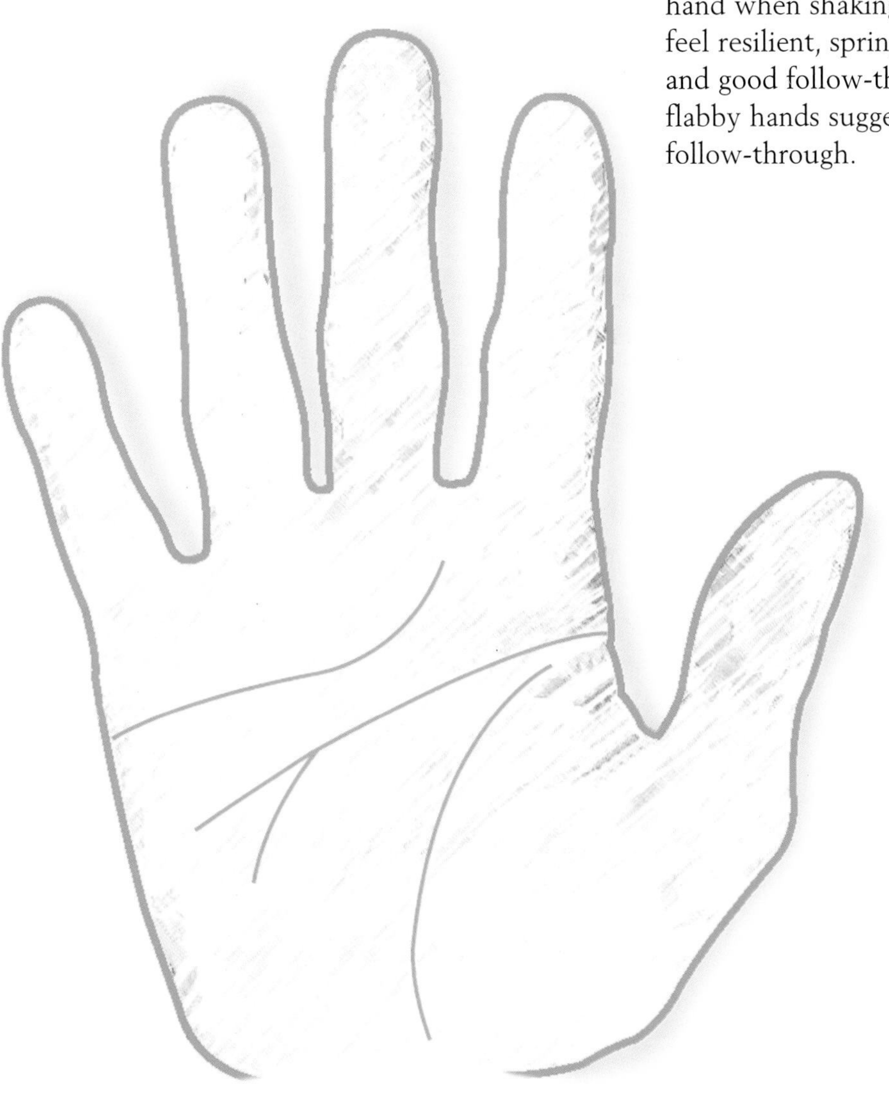

Tone

Tone refers to the overall "feel" of another's hand when shaking it or holding it. Palms that feel resilient, springy, and elastic suggest vitality and good follow-through. Soft, "lifeless," or flabby hands suggest a lack of energy and poor follow-through.

Part II
The Fingers

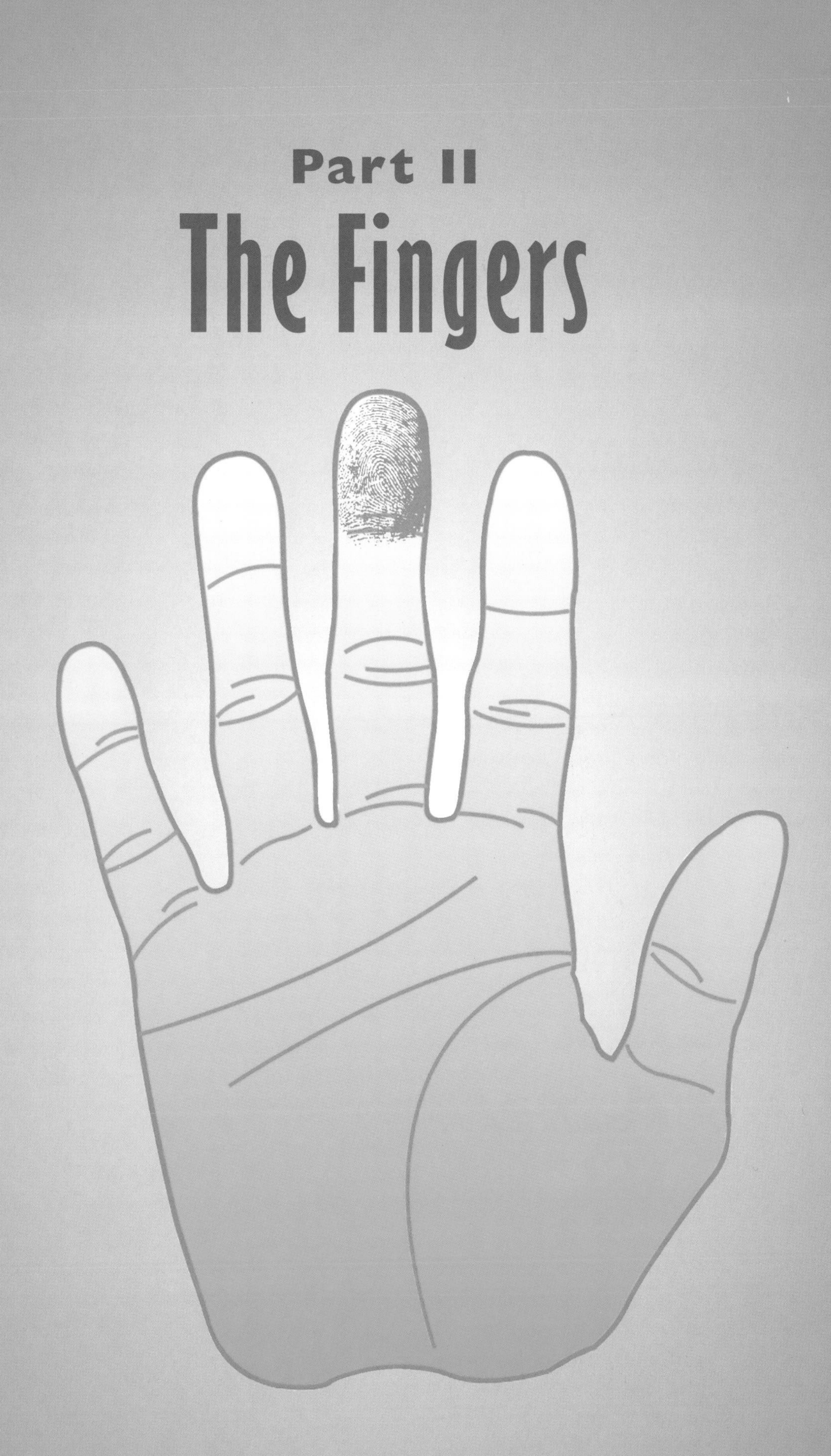

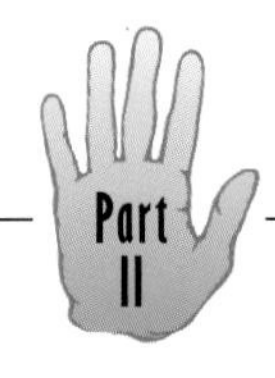

General Characteristics

To get a general picture of who you are, palmists look at the overall finger characteristics. For more specific information, they examine each finger individually.

Flexibility

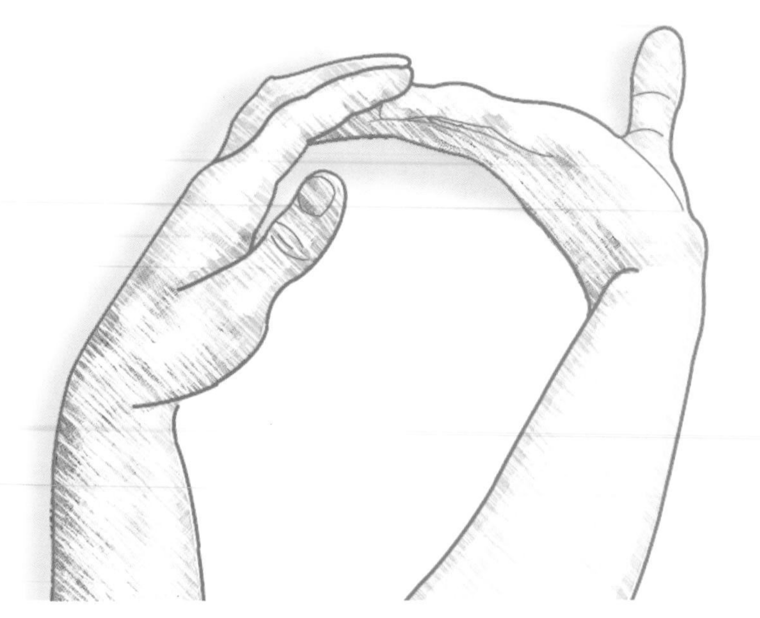

The degree of flexibility in your fingers tells how adaptable you are. The general rule is, the more rigid the fingers are when they are gently pressed backward, the less open-minded you are. Ideally fingers should arch gently under pressure. If yours don't, it might mean that you don't like to admit you're wrong or that you refuse to see the other person's side of the story. When your fingers flex way back, arching easily, you'll do anything to avoid an argument.

Length

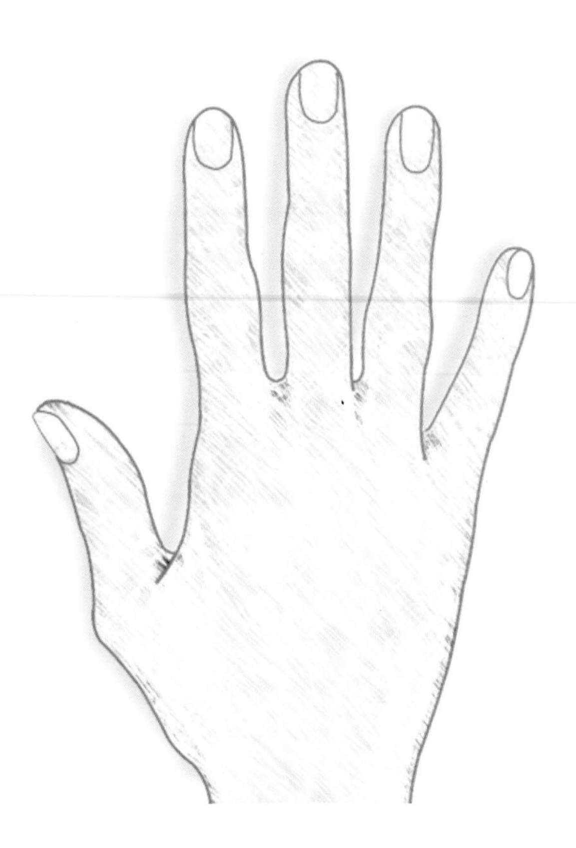

Finger length is judged in relation to the length of the palm itself and is gauged by looking at the hand fingernail-side up.

Long Fingers

Do your fingers appear long in relation to your palm? People with long fingers take their time doing things and tend to fuss over the whys and hows of a job. Planning, analyzing, discussing, and asking questions are important. You enjoy assessing and categorizing situations. You don't fear demonstrating emotions or affection. Security to you means understanding a situation and having it so well scoped out that you can explain it to anybody. You have an instinct for putting yourself into another's shoes.

You consider yourself equal to anybody and want to be respected for your mind rather than your status or good looks. The ultimate individualist, you can't bear to have anyone else force you or tell you how to do anything. You feel lost when you can't come up with a solution or alternative plan. Once you get going, it's hard to keep up with you because you don't easily run out of steam. You like being the instigator. You'd rather be ruined by praise than saved by criticism. Don't kill the messenger or dismiss what is said—criticism doesn't mean that others are always right. Be open.

Long Palms

A long palm with long fingers. You enjoy talking things out but may get hung up on small details and miss the big picture. Much of your energy goes into mental activity, and you are passionate about your ideas. Intuitive and sensitive to others, you're full of empathy. You probably have a strong voice and can put a great deal into what you say. Unfortunately you frequently put others first, ignoring your own best interests. You have a tendency to burn out through stress and mental strain, and might need to force yourself to get more exercise.

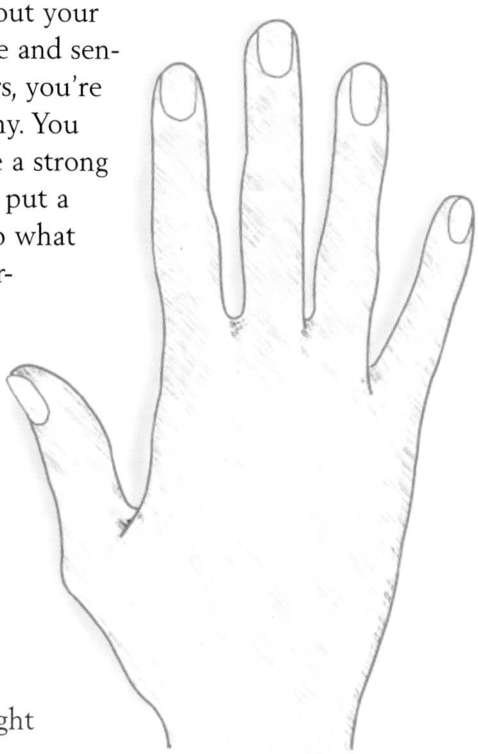

A bit high-strung with lots of nervous energy, you're not an aggressive or overly physical person. You work well in creative arenas. Your ability to grow and expand your field of influence is unlimited. But you aren't looking for glory or prestige—you're content to work behind the scenes. You should look for a career with unlim-ited growth potential. Routine occupations would deny you the chance to make full use of your creativity and imagination.

A long palm with short fingers. You are someone who tends to be argumentative. You often make up your mind before all the facts are on the table. You are impatient with your emotions and those of others. To you, feelings are stumbling blocks that get in the way of things you want to do. Anger and irritability come easily, but you don't stay mad for very long because you want to move on to the next thing. An extrovert at times, you're well suited to careers that involve change, assertiveness, and adventure.

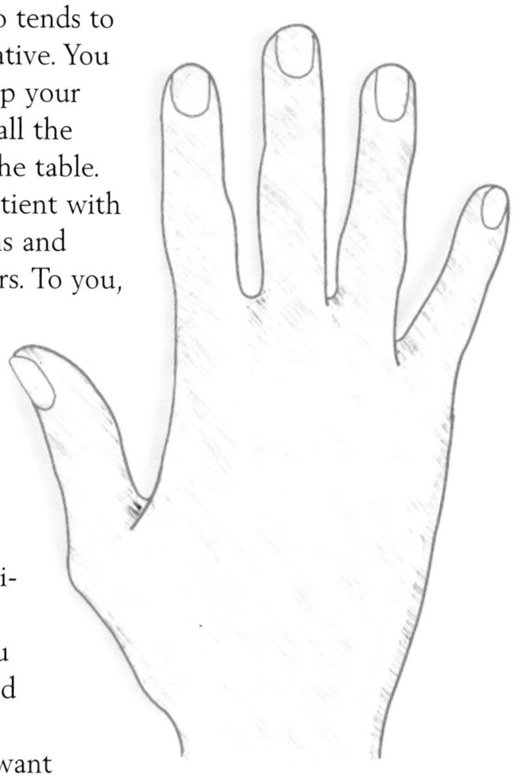

Although you may consider yourself humble and not a natural leader, you project an image of confidence and self-sufficiency. Hard-working and conscientious, you focus all of your energy to do a task well. You uphold the rights and well-being of others, though you may be unwilling to fight for yourself. It's maddening and frustrating when people don't believe what we say, but your actions speak louder than words. Follow up what you say and don't tolerate aggressive intimidation. You'll gain credibility walking your talk.

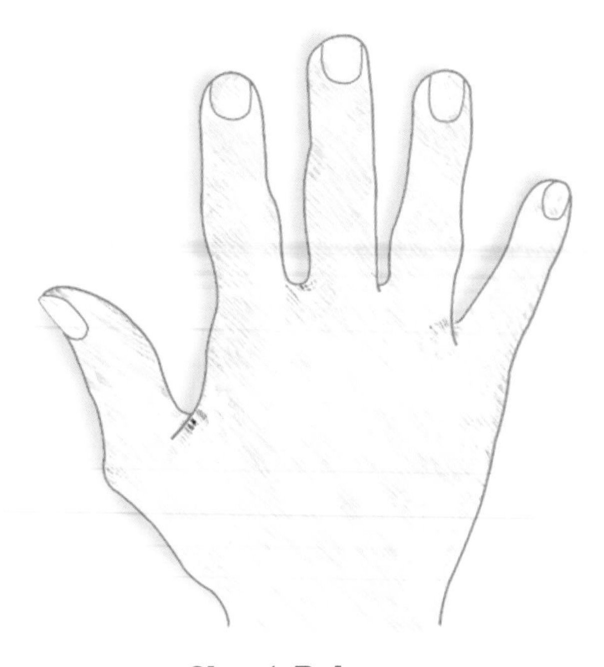

Short, square palm with long fingers

Short Palms

A short, square palm with short fingers. You are one of those down-to-earth, logical souls who work well in the daily grind of the material world. Preferring a stable and predictable life-style, you dislike change. You're self-sufficient and aggressive about what you need. Punctual and straightforward, you see things in an uncomplicated manner and may enjoy a career in agriculture or horticulture, mechanical fields, or accounting, jobs where the focus is on one task at a time.

Instead of moving outwardly with vigor and force, you often hold your energy in check. Your common sense and managerial ability are good at organizing others and delegating responsibility, although you may have a difficult time firing anyone. Risks are difficult for you because you're overly cautious and economically aware. You may have trouble breaking old habits or traditions to try new avenues, but action talks louder than fear or any other raging emotion.

A short, square palm with long fingers. This reveals someone who's mentally alert, insatiabley curious, and ready to exchange opinions with others. Like a detective, you are amused and stimulated by putting a puzzle together. You emphasize levelheaded thinking, clear language, and careful research, and you take the time to explain things well. You are street-smart, have no fear of intellectual challenge, and enjoy outspoken people.

Material possessions and creature comforts are important to you, and you'll do whatever you can to acquire them in abundance. Once you decide on something, you are not easily distracted or discouraged, and you often succeed because of your single-minded persistence. Normally a well-mannered diplomat, you try to avoid arguments and rarely lose your temper. You weigh your words carefully and make clearheaded, fact-based judgments, without letting your feelings intrude. Communications, teaching, publishing, and public relations are ideal fields for you.

Very Short Fingers

Do your fingers appear very short in relation to your palm? Short-fingered folk act on matters quickly and understand the larger scheme of things. Unfortunately you don't always take time to think things through. Your abrupt and occasionally reckless actions can have disastrous consequences. Your mental grasp is greater than its depth.

Always in a rush, you tend to overlook details. On the other hand, your pioneering spirit is strong, and no failure can discourage you. Goals that can be achieved quickly are better choices for you than ones that require years of planning. You may have trouble accepting praise for what you do, and may perform tasks so modestly that others don't always notice what you do for them. Stand tall, speak loud! Our greatest glory consists not in constant success, but in rising every time we come up short.

Shape

There are four major finger shapes: thick, thin, knobby, and smooth, each representing a different personality trait. Most people's hands have one dominant finger shape. Some hands, however, may have a combination of finger shapes, which signifies versatility.

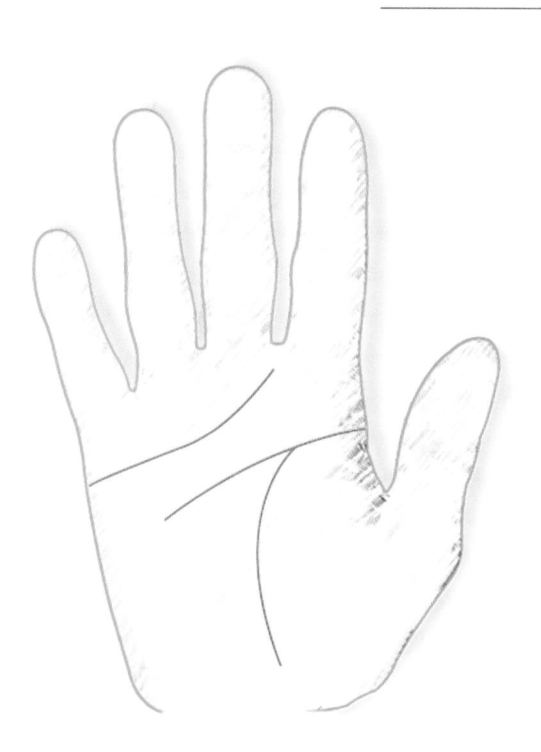

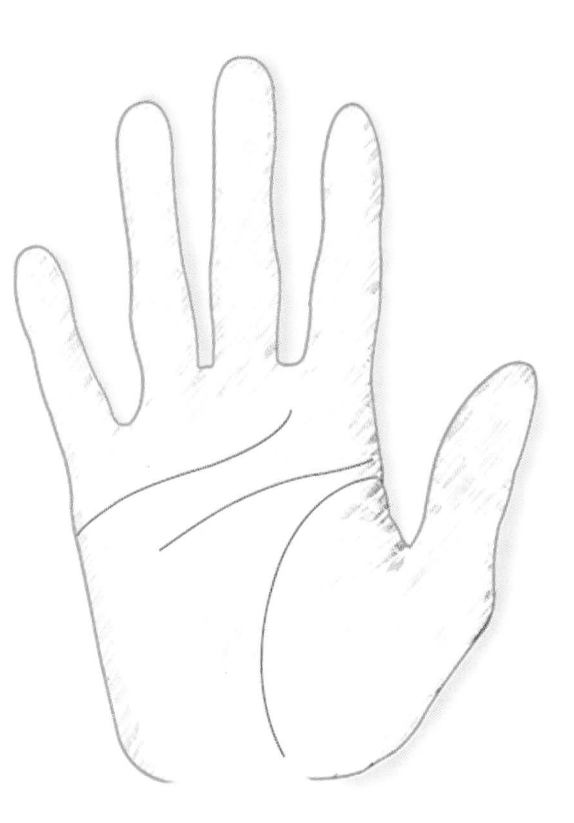

Thick, Fleshy Fingers

This shape reveals a sensual person. You yearn to touch, feel, see, hear, and taste all that life has to offer. You enjoy good food and luxury, and you may be a bit of a couch potato. But you do want to be productive and transfer your interests into material form—you may not always be content to admire the creations of others. You can be stubborn, but you usually can set your ego aside when teamwork or compromise is called for.

You have a penchant for having and doing things your way. Beware of prejudice or becoming a workaholic! Enjoy. Relax. One thing you are likely to pursue is wealth, and you'll invest much effort to this end. Material possessions and things that make you "feel" good are necessary for personal happiness. Real joy flows from neither riches nor praise, but from doing something worthwhile.

Thin Fingers

You always take time to think things through. You weigh the pros and cons of a situation and make factual judgments without being overly influenced by your feelings. You debate issues cleverly but avoid becoming emotionally involved. You are dramatic and creative. You love to preach. But one likes being preached at, even if you inspire others. Lower your voice; live and let live.

You get turned on by what lurks beneath the surface, and you seek security, stability, and an orderly, well-defined life. Upholding the status quo enhances your own status. As part of the establishment, you are likely to increase your wealth and sense of security. A career in communications or working with young people would be a good choice to provide you the feedback you need.

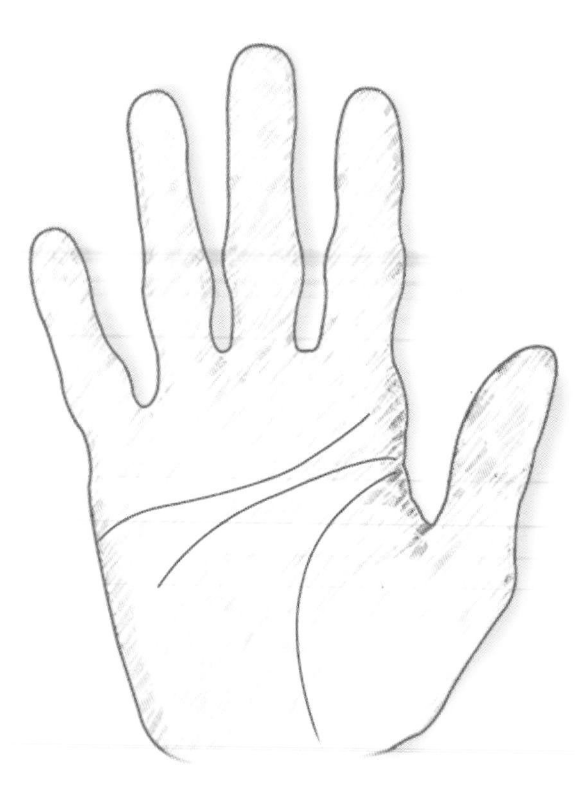

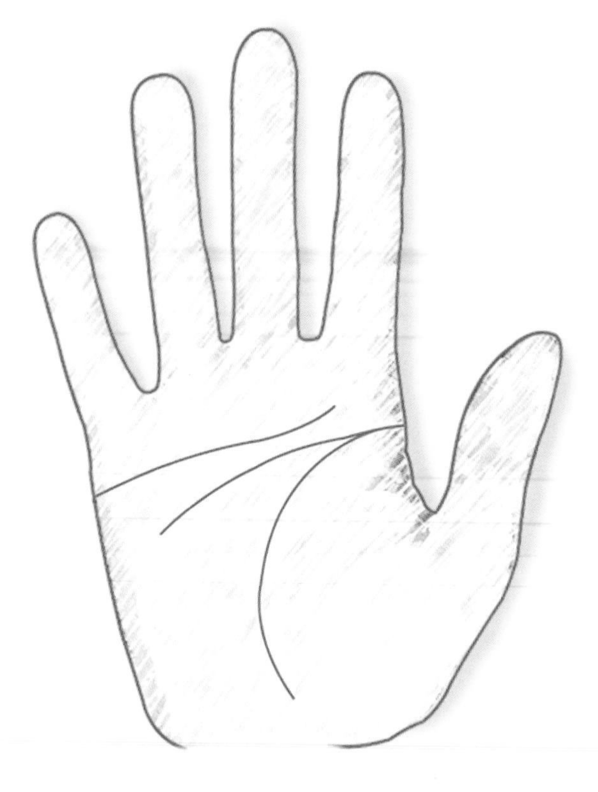

Knobby Fingers

You are a problem-solver who thinks logically, taking time to weigh the pros and cons of any action or situation. Large knuckles, also called "knots," suggest objectivity and patience. You don't like disagreements, and because you want to maintain stability in your emotional life, you don't express your dissatisfactions easily. Success comes to you because you never think about failing. Life guarantees a chance—not always a fair shake.

Smooth Fingers

You play your hunches instead of following conventional wisdom. Your passions usually rule your thinking, yet you rarely act in haste or in anger. You often have difficulty asserting yourself and going after what you want in a direct manner. Because love is vital to your happiness, you place more emphasis on your partner or relationship than on yourself.

You feel a kinship to all living things and can't bear to see any creature suffer. Your extreme sensitivity to people and to your environment may frighten you and make you vulnerable or defenseless. Since you are deeply affected by your surroundings and injustice, you must learn to use this sensitivity constructively, perhaps in painting, writing, or composing.

Specific Characteristics

Each finger is named after an ancient mythological deity or one of the planets, and each tells a different story. The fingers are like a quintet of musicians—each plays a different tune.

The Index Finger: Jupiter

Jupiter reveals your assertiveness and leadership abilities. When it's short—not reaching above the top joint of the middle finger—you're easily intimidated.

When the index finger is nearly the same length as the ring finger. You enjoy being in control. Because you dislike taking orders from anyone, you would do well to be self-employed. You possess a strong sense of the dramatic and can be flamboyant in the way you express yourself. Subtlety is unknown to you. You tend to magnify your emotions and have a taste for the larger-than-life. You have a strong yearning for praise and applause, and no fear of hard work. You are confident you can get whatever you want, and you probably will.

When the index finger is shorter than the ring finger. You would rather follow than lead. You gain emotional satisfaction from being helpful and like to feel needed. You would rather not be the center of attention nor have too many responsibilities. You're extraordinarily sensitive and are easily hurt. This may sometimes lead you to take a backseat to others.

Conservative and spiritual, you are inclined to follow established philosophies and traditional faiths. You can't stand to see suffering. Your keen sensitivity enables you to feel kinship with all living things. You like to be useful and have the best intentions to help others, but may lack the courage to follow through. Avoid feeling that your efforts are futile if you don't see evidence of your effectiveness. Sometimes your contribution is low-key, though high in value.

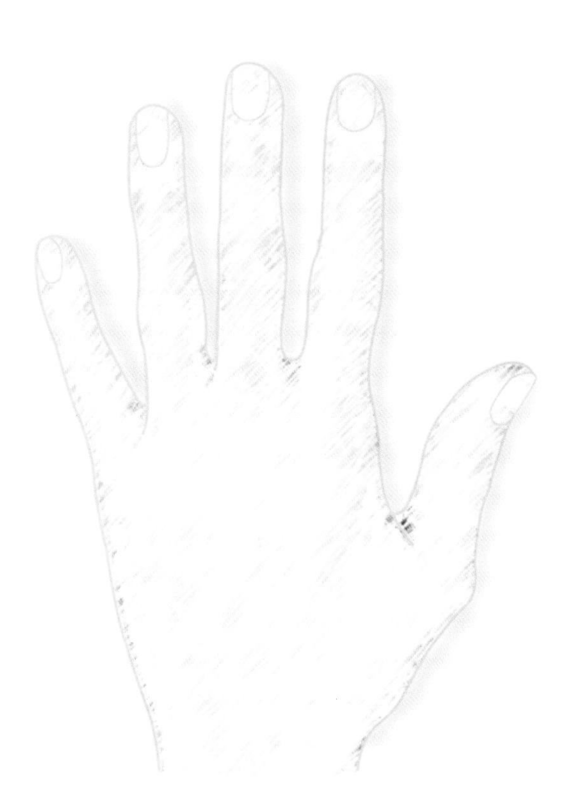

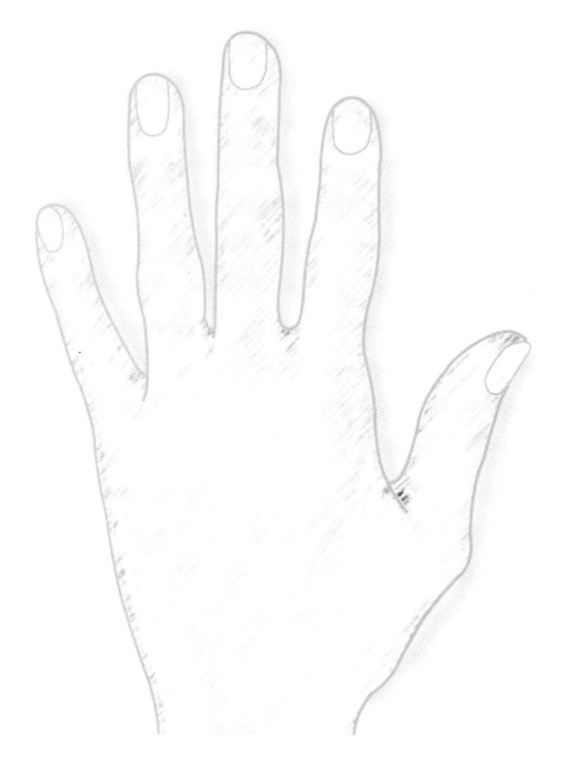

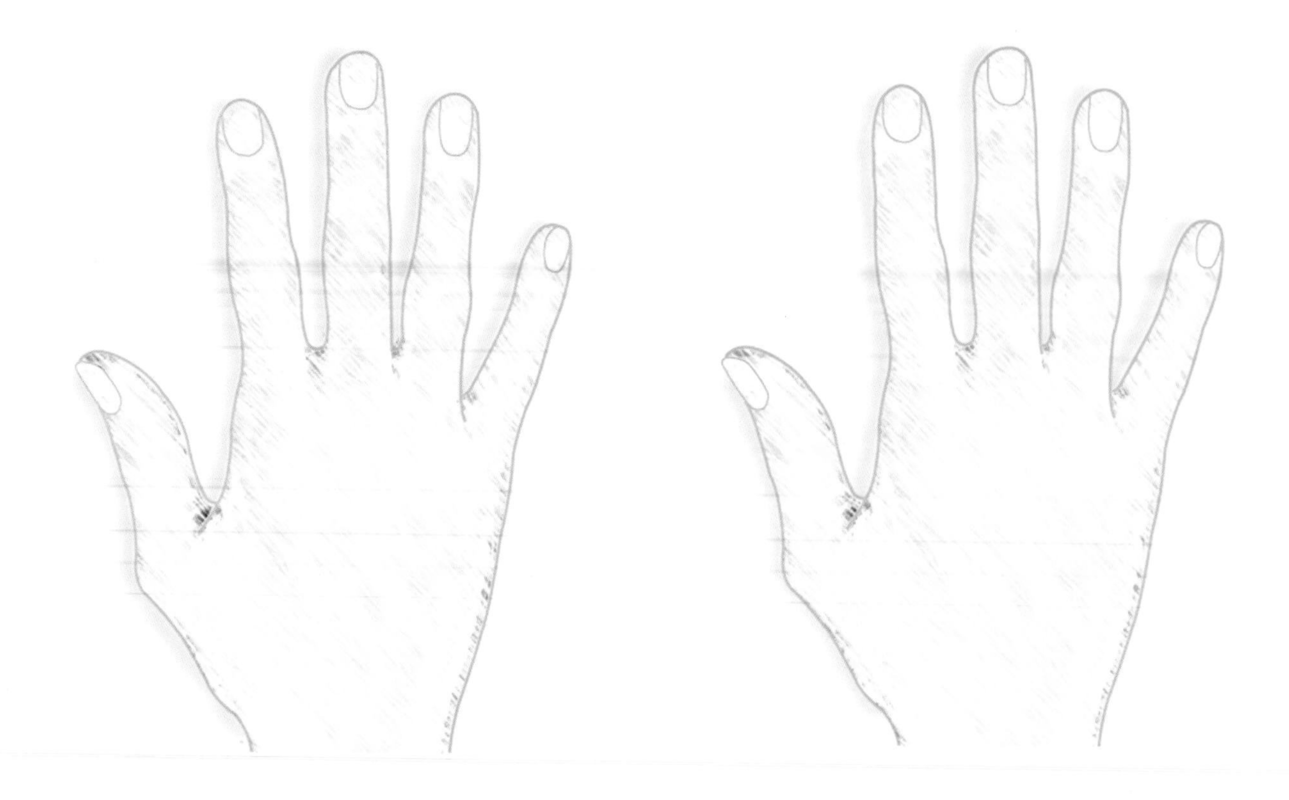

When the index fingertip leans away from the middle finger. You project an image of confidence and vitality that makes others immediately notice you. However, you can be arrogant or vain. In your self-concern, you often fail to realize the needs of others and thus turn off the various admirers whose respect you so desperately desire. You are always ready to accept praise for your accomplishments, but rarely take the blame for any failures. In your long climb to succeed, don't forget those who helped you get there.

When the index finger reaches above the nail bed of the middle finger, when viewed from the back of the hand. This suggests star quality and strong self-confidence. The ultimate individualist, you can't bear to have anyone tell you what to do or how to do it. You test your own limits and firmly believe you never know what you can accomplish until you try.

Choose a career that affords you an opportunity to grow and develop, because you are sure of yourself and what you can accomplish. You take pride in yourself and your achievements. You're tough to ignore when you have something to say, have a strong sense of self, and always seek new ways to do things.

The Middle Finger: Saturn

Saturn reflects how you learn and how you take to discipline.

When the middle finger is long and straight. This reveals a love for schedules. You're serious about your commitments and don't mind being alone. Work is very important to you, and you're happiest when situations are orderly and structured. You possess natural managerial abilities and are known for shrewdness, diligence, and reliability. Although you are ambitious, status and recognition are not as important to you as honor and personal happiness.

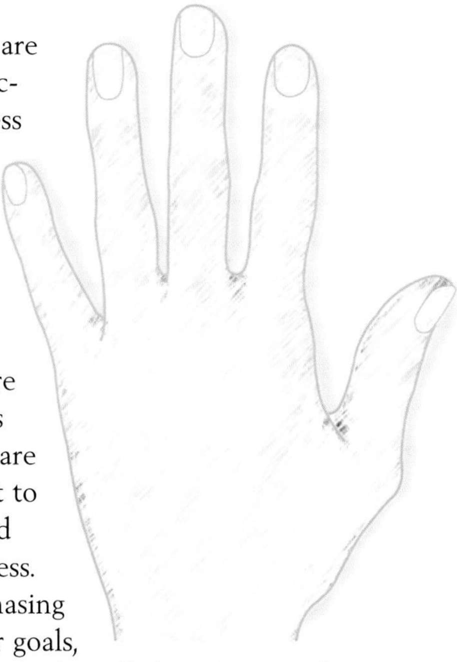

Instead of chasing madly after your goals, you pursue them with well-thought-out plans and dogged determination. When something needs to get done, you're the one to do it, and you accomplish more than most through efficient, practical organization of your time. Working makes you feel good about yourself, and your ego is gratified by feeling that you're indispensable.

When a middle finger reaches only the top of the ring finger, when viewed palm up. You tend to be old-fashioned and conservative, and you like to stick to what you know instead of taking chances on new ideas or practices. You hold onto your resources and prefer to make it on your own, never relying on others. Taking risks is difficult for you.

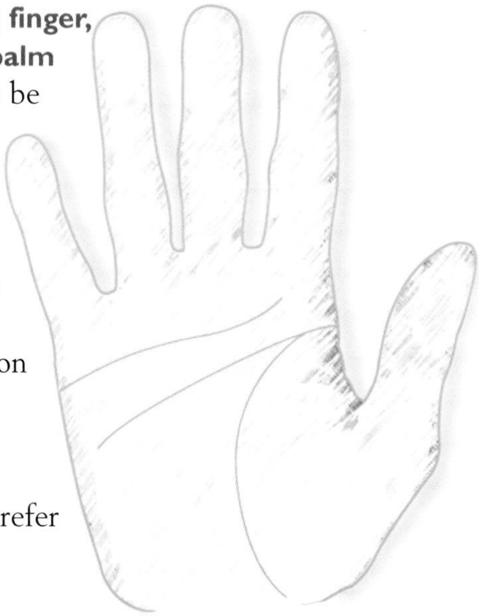

When the middle finger is bent or curved. The sign of the collector, one who hoards and saves. Your physical home and personal belongings represent security and stability to you. Highly critical of yourself, you might be inclined to undervalue your abilities. Guard against carrying your need to own things to extremes.

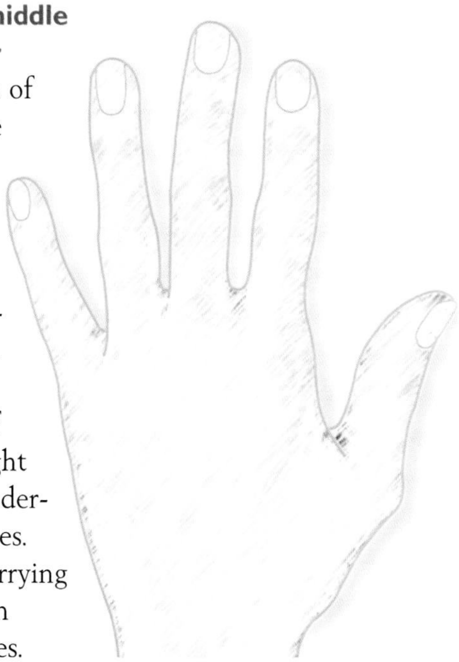

When the middle finger has large knuckles. Learning and scholarly pursuits are your greatest skills. You have plenty of common sense about finances but have trouble remembering where you left your car keys. You're defensive about your rights and sometimes fear that your independence will be hindered. People are impressed with your ability to assert yourself and challenge any rule that interferes with your desires.

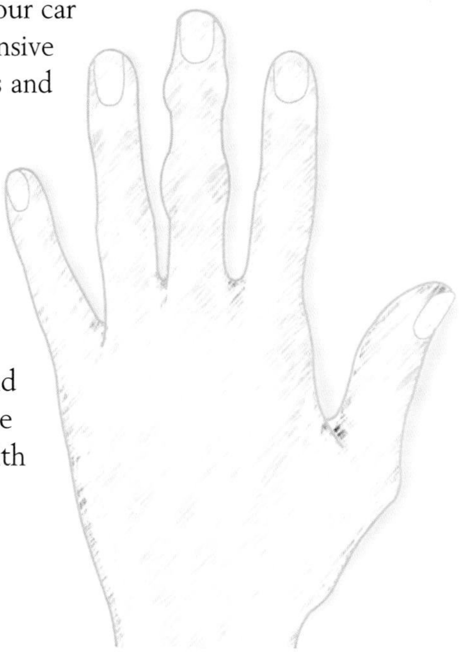

The Ring Finger: Venus

Venus, the ring finger, speaks of your personal style, capacity for joy, happiness with work, and appreciation of the arts.

When the ring finger nearly reaches the tip of the middle finger. Watch your checking account, because your eyes are bigger than your bank balance when it comes to money management. This is the sign of the gambler! Watch your wallet! You're a lover, not an accountant.

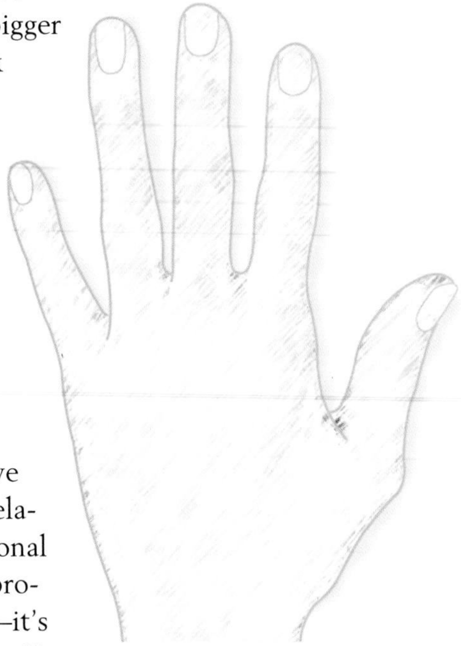

Once you've established a relationship—personal more so than professional ones—it's likely to endure. You are willing to work long and hard to make relationships strong and lasting. Tactful and refined, you are concerned with saying and doing the "right" things. Diplomacy is your middle name. You can't bear anger, hostility, or conflict, nor can you stand to have others mad at you. You vacillate when faced with big decisions. In your professional life, you're more content working in groups than by yourself.

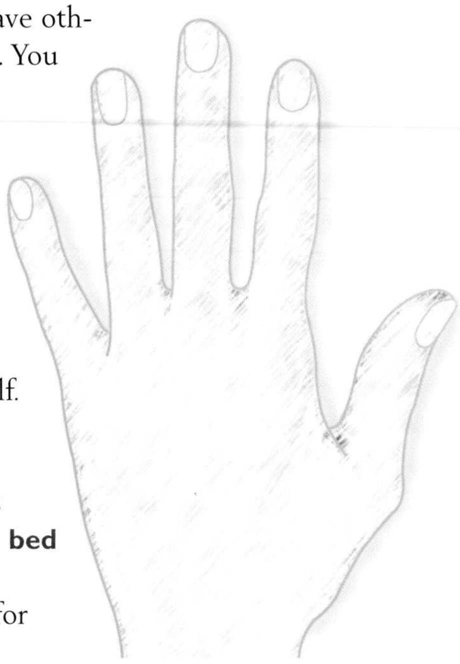

When a straight ring finger reaches above the nail bed of the middle finger. Caring for someone makes your world safe and desirable. The emotional attachments you make are strong and enduring. Friends and family mean more to you than approval from co-workers, employers,and strangers. A difference of opinion or lifestyle seems downright dangerous to you. You view others as either with you or against you.

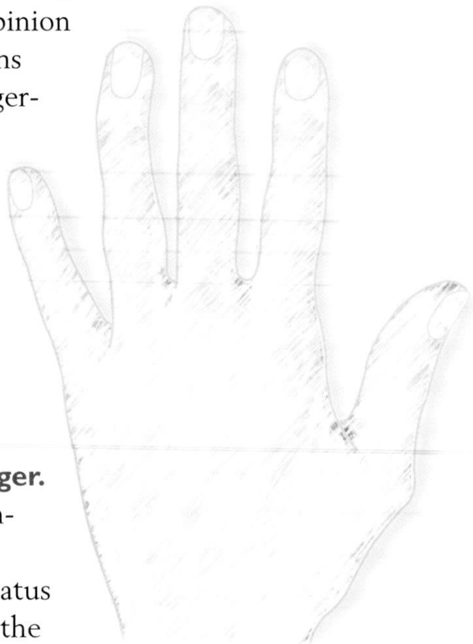

When the ring fingertip bends toward the middle finger. You're very concerned about approval and status quo. Following the rules and keeping up with the Joneses are important.

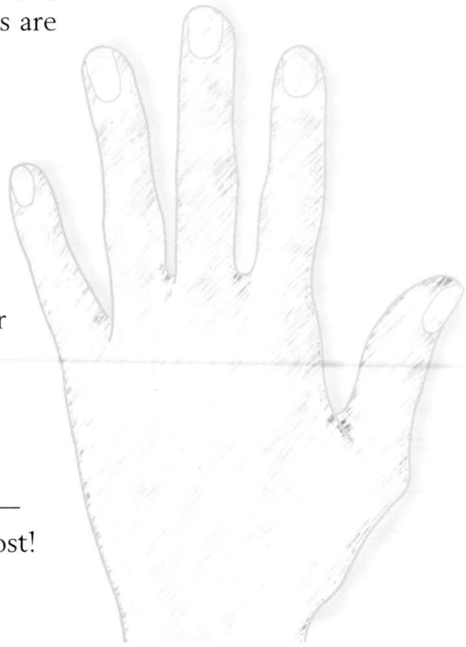

When it leans toward the little finger. You like to do things your way and at your own pace. Always considerate and rarely rebellious, your opinion counts—first and foremost!

The Little Finger: Mercury

Mercury, the little finger, deals with how you learn and communicate. In ancient mythology he was the messenger between mortals and gods; in palm reading this digit is associated with all forms of verbal exchange—such as speaking and writing.

When the little finger reaches above the ring finger's top knuckle. You think big and talk well. Optimistic and adventuresome, your enthusiasm is contagious. Your mind is always seeking, always active. You're a storehouse of facts and trivia. You're pretty good as a money manager. You learn quickly and demonstrate an eagerness to get things done. Those with long little fingers make fine speakers, singers, and musicians.

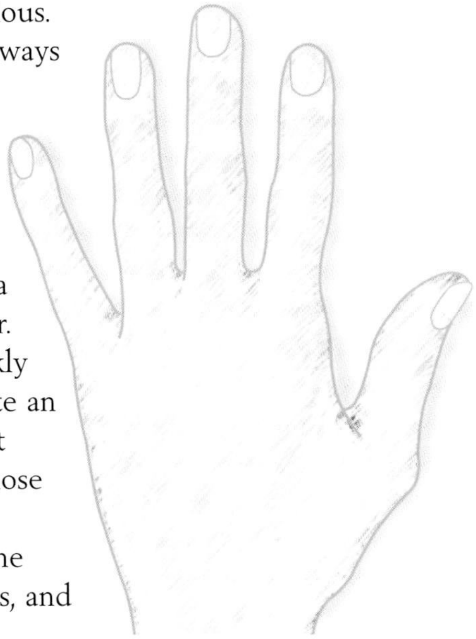

So many ideas vie for your attention that you could have trouble holding focus. A lifelong student, you never stop learning. However, it's easy for you to scatter your energies and get overwhelmed by projects. Try one thing at a time. You may have more ideas than you realize for changing social values and inspiring others. Follow your heart and take things one day, and step, at a time.

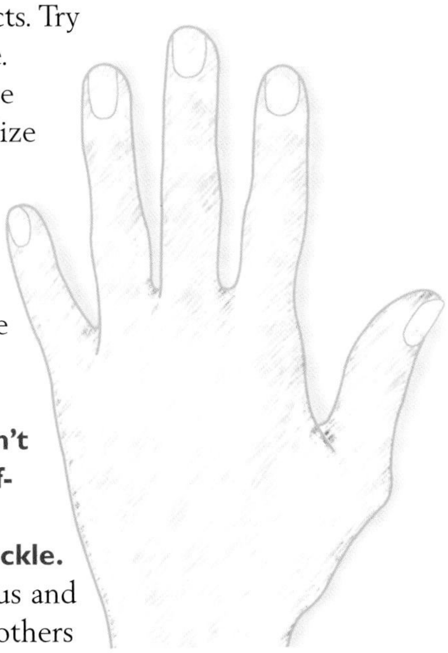

When it doesn't reach at least halfway up the ring finger's lower knuckle. You are mischievous and clever but rely on others to do the dirty work. Quick-thinking and sly as Tom Sawyer and conniving as Huckleberry Finn, you understand how to get others to do unto you. You don't work well on your own.

When the little finger naturally leans away from the ring finger. This suggests an inability to get along with people. Your focus on details often causes you to miss the larger picture. Once you relax and realize that everyone has failings, you'll improve your chances for satisfactory relationships.

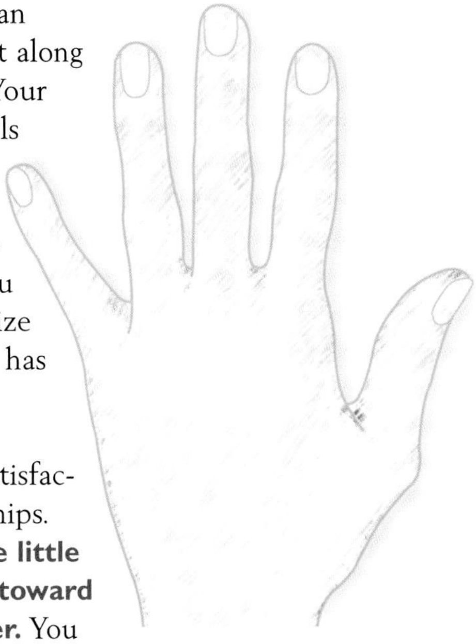

When the little finger bends toward the ring finger. You care for other people and for m-o-n-e-y. Finances play an important role in your daily life, but you're always there to help. "How much is this going to cost me?" is your catchphrase.

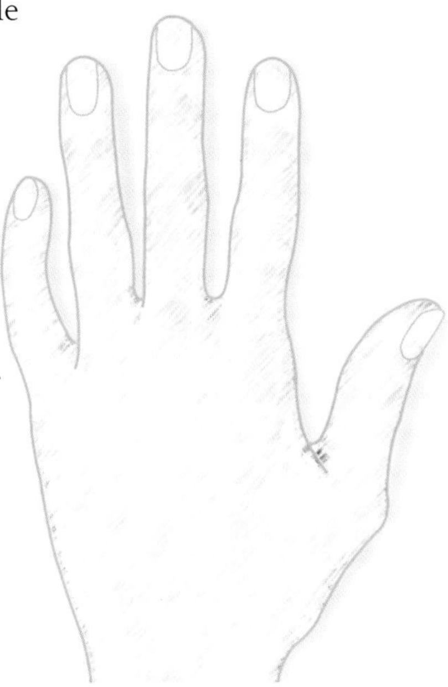

The Thumb: Uranus

The thumb, called Uranus, spells out individuality, self-determination and perseverance, open-mindedness and willingness to change, and a sense of self-worth.

The elevated mount at its base—called the Mount of the Sun—bespeaks physical energy and ego; the nail section indicates strength of willpower; and the in-between area, called the bottom phalange, relates to intelligence and logic.

When the thumb has a high, firm Mount of the Sun. This indicates a strong will and sense of confidence. You are an active, energetic, and sensual person—a real go-getter.

When the thumb has a flat Mount of the Sun. You yearn for consistency and security. You prefer to surround yourself with people who think like you. Watch out for intimidation from others. Take a firm stand when you know you're right. Don't feel obligated to others who try to take advantage of your compassionate nature. Establish goals within your abilities and stop doubting that you'll be able to score.

When the tip of the thumb arches freely backward. You do what others tell you and are concerned about what the neighbors think. Your heart rules your head, and you may have trouble making rational decisions. Don't let others take advantage of your generosity! You tend to deliver more than requested. Make a realistic appraisal of what you need and devise a plan to achieve it.

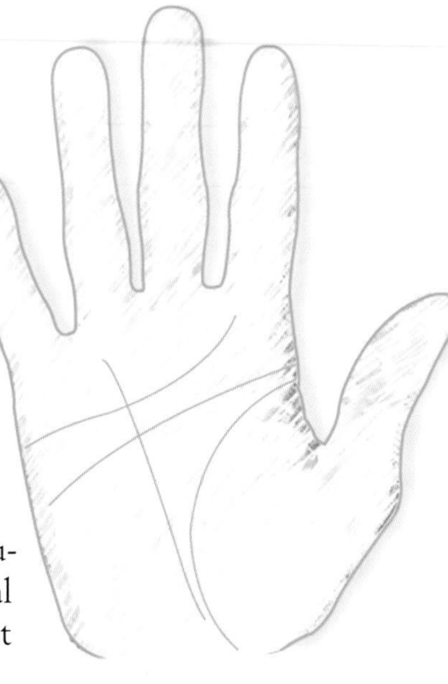

When the thumb is thick and inflexible. This belongs to someone who prefers working in structured, impersonal, and unemotional environments. Cautious and conservative, you are inclined to stick with tried-and-true methods. Beware of becoming a workaholic: learn to balance work with play. Stop worrying about problems that never arise.

When the thumb naturally falls away from the fingers. A 45-degree or wider angle between the thumb and the side of your hand reveals a generous, open-minded person willing to compromise and consider the options for all concerned. Ideas and concepts are important to you. You respect intelligence and individuality but are more concerned with theory than application. Your quick wit and humor make you very charismatic.

You make the most of opportunities to demonstrate your creative talents, but you do so without alienating competitors. You assert yourself positively when you encounter resistance to your plans. Your understanding of people and their problems offers numerous opportunities for professional success.

When your thumb naturally hugs the side of the hand. You don't like to do things spontaneously. You're goal-oriented and like to have plenty of time to plan your moves carefully. You're a good judge of character, and your understanding of people gives you advantages in realizing your personal and professional objectives. You feel that most difficulties can be resolved through good communications. People with problems depend on you because they know you can show them how to make better use of their time and resources.

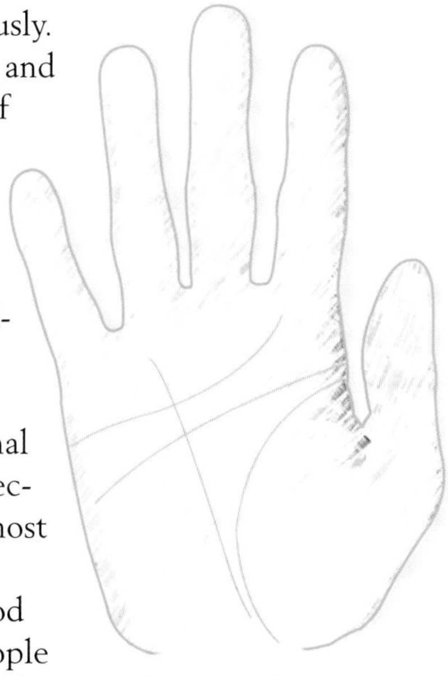

When your thumb reaches the middle joint of the index finger. This is a sign of solid self-esteem and willingness to help others. You're always ready with a word of encouragement and feel genuinely joyous when making people happy. You feel secure in a command position. You seem never to grow tired and frequently burn the candle at both ends. Pride keeps you from being overly dependent on others. Rarely do others thumb their nose at you.

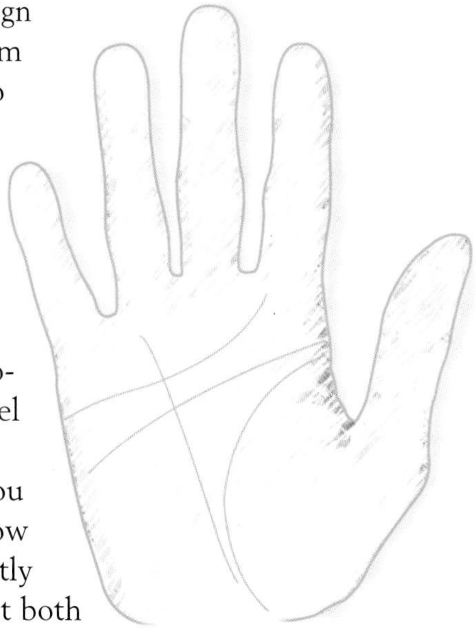

When your thumb doesn't reach the bottom of the index finger. You're short on willpower and follow-through. You have problems making up your mind. It's difficult for you to separate yourself from other's needs and desires. Too compassionate, you don't know how or when to draw the line with people who cling to you. You're easy to get along with, but you've got to learn to say no.

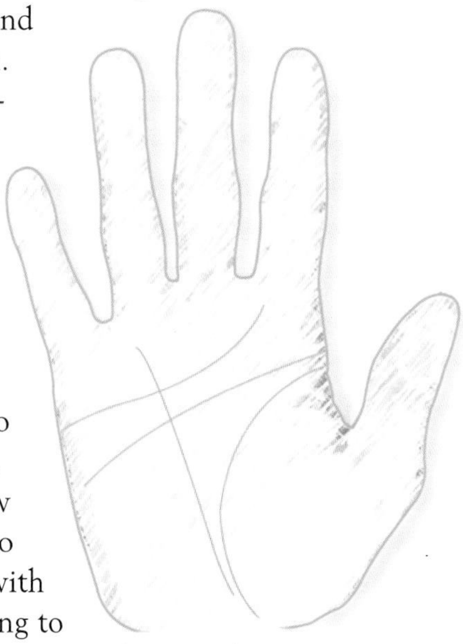

When your thumb is inflexible and stiff-tipped. You are argumentative and overly set in your ways. You pride yourself on getting the job done, but you like to get it done your way. You rarely take chances with time or money. Your friendships may be few, but they are usually forever.

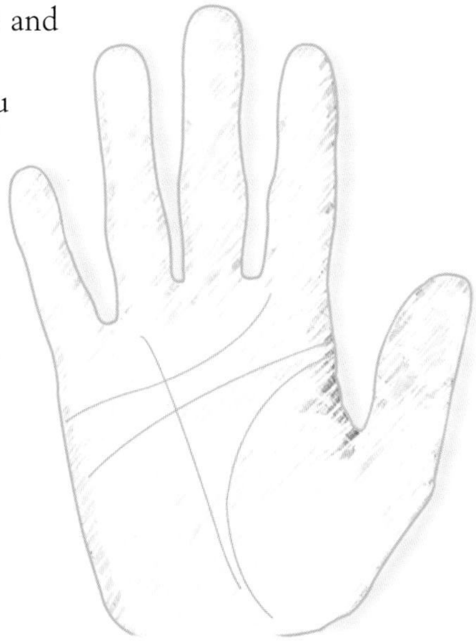

The Phalanges

Fingers have three sections and thumbs two called phalanges (*fuh-lan-geez*), marked by deep horizontal lines when viewed from the palm. Normally each of these sections is unequal in length. The base section, closest to the palm, deals with sensuality; the middle with practical efforts; the top with intellect and spirituality. Consider the traits of each finger when examining them, noting which is longest and which is widest.

In general, when the bottom phalange is puffy you have a love of physical satisfactions. When it's thin or flat you're hard-working but prefer working in groups. Delicacy or weakness prevails when it has a "waist"—like the middle of an hourglass.

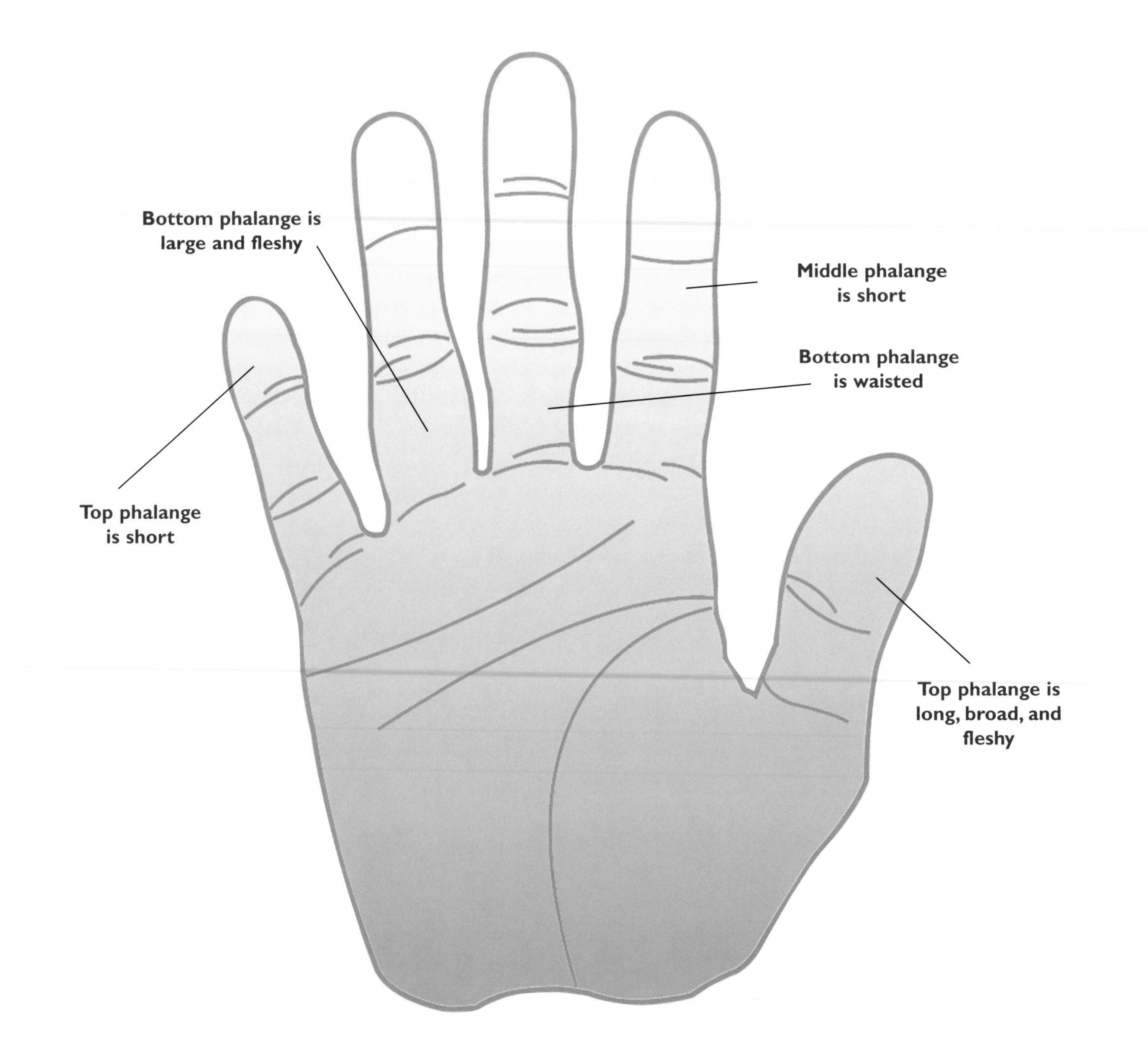

The Index Finger

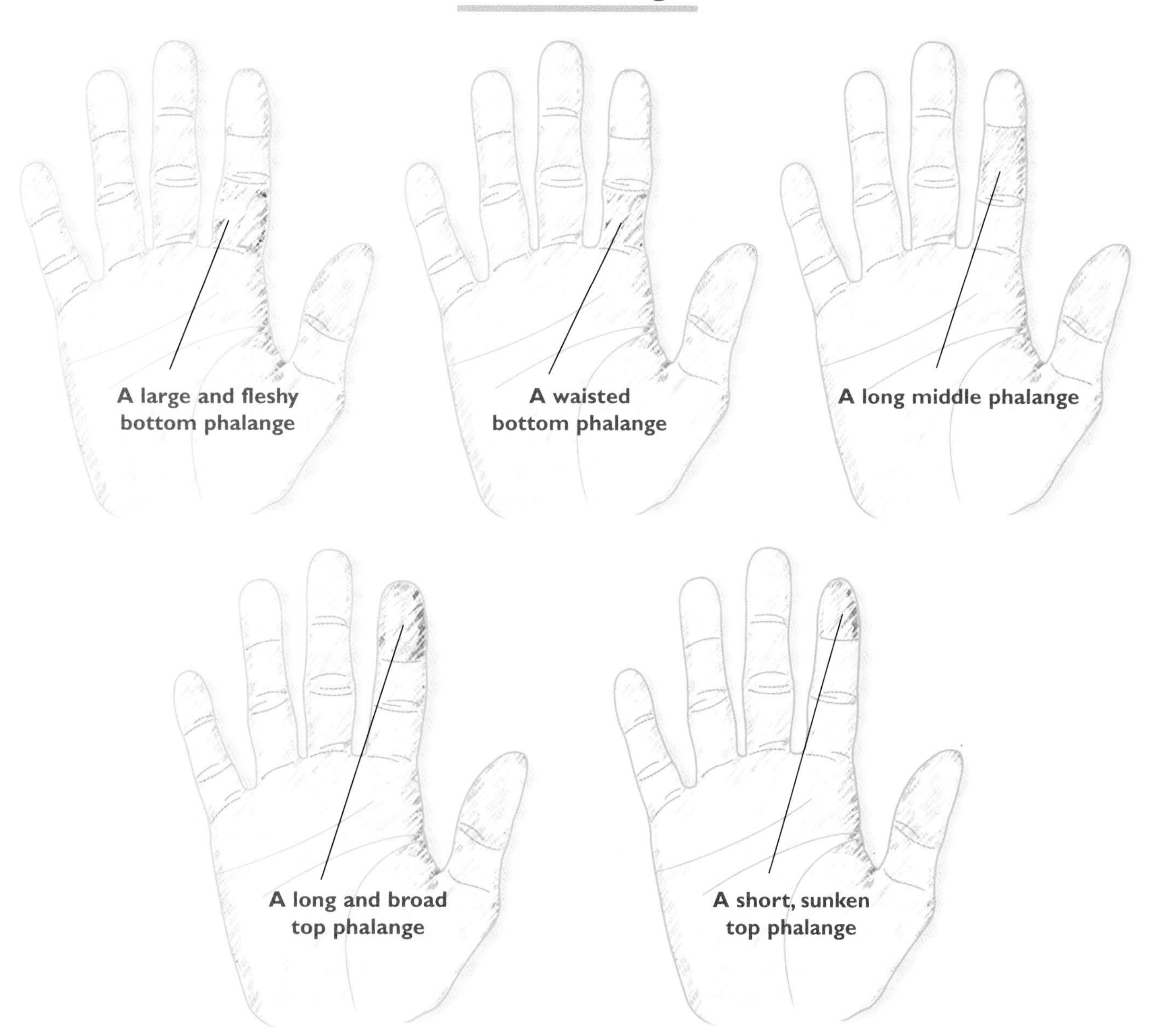

When the bottom phalange is large and fleshy. This suggests gourmet tastes and a love of luxury. You express yourself in physical terms and love creature comforts. You enjoy touching and being touched. You use your sensory awareness to expand your understanding of the world and your place in it. You're a lover of life and beautiful things.

When the bottom phalange is waisted. This suggests fast food and little physical activity. You seek simple pleasures and have humble needs.

When the middle phalange is long, broad, or fleshy. You have an aptitude for crafts, practical improvements, or domestic work. Exactitude and playing by the rules are your loves.

When the top phalange is long, broad, or fleshy. You have high morals, dignity, and integrity. Traditionall, this is the sign of a priest or holy person. You think of others' welfare first.

When the top phalange is short, sunken, or waisted. You prefer learning by reading or cassette tapes—impersonal exchanges rather than one on one. Structured, unemotional environments suit you best.

The Middle Finger

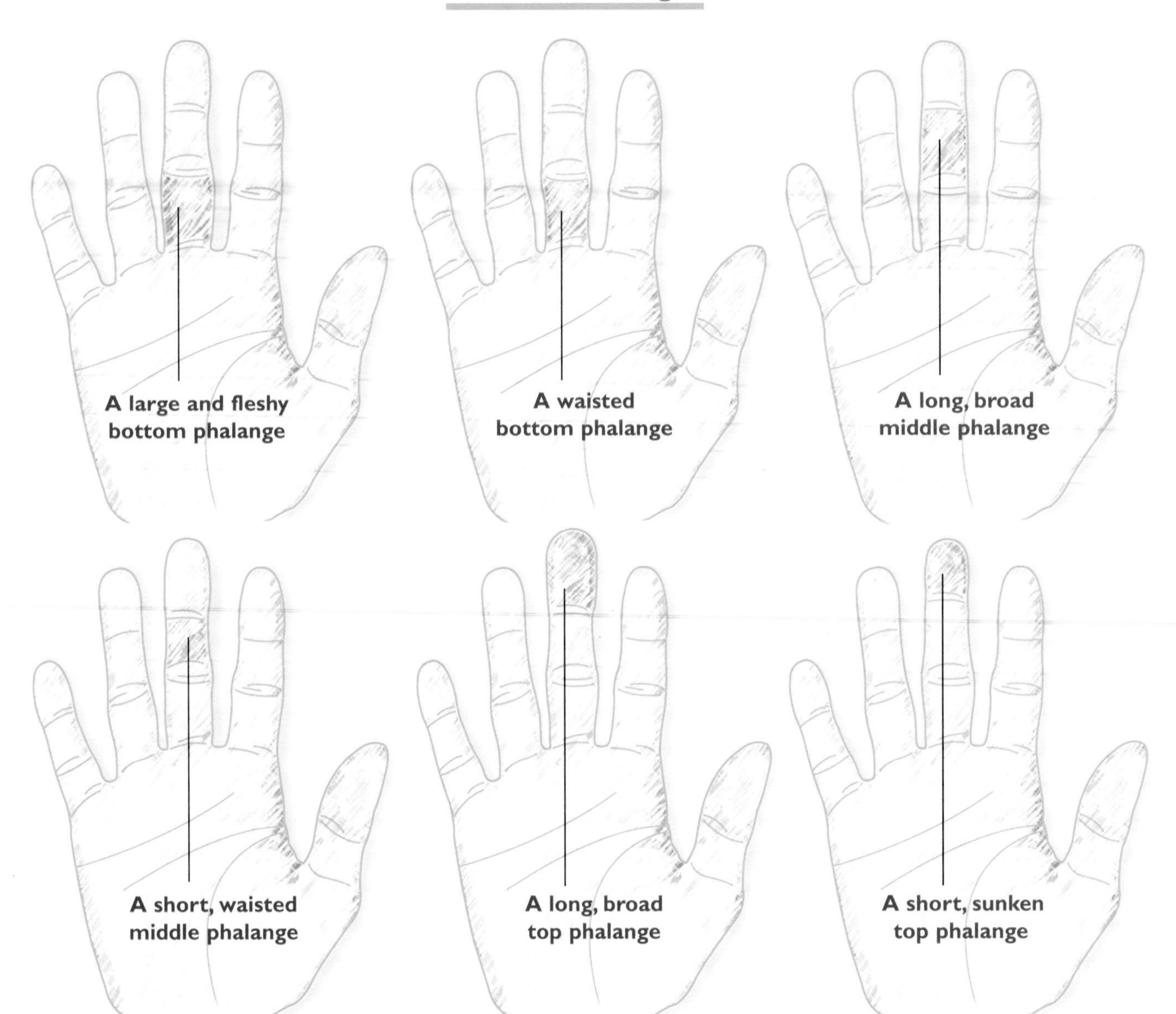

When the bottom phalange is large and fleshy. You'd be happy as a gardener or farmer. Cooking from scratch, home canning, and doing what comes naturally make you happiest. Family and home mean more to you than friends and social status. You're a staunch defender of domestic rights.

When the bottom phalange is waisted. You may have trouble seeing your family as individuals rather than as extensions of yourself. Security conscious, you often imagine threats that are not real. Inclined to let your heart rule your head, you have trouble making rational, detached decisions.

When the middle phalange is long, broad, or fleshy. You are aware of society's rules and etiquette and play things by the book. You are never eccentric or rebellious, and traditional morals and values suit you best.

When the middle phalange is short or waisted. You are easily intimidated and have trouble saying no. Prioritizing is problematic. You're happiest working with partners.

When the top phalange is long, broad, or fleshy. You have a good intellect and a need to look beneath the surface of matters. Self-sufficient, you don't rely on others. Beware of pride or snobbishness.

When the top phalange is short, sunken, or waisted. You must guard against perfectionism. Rigid in your thinking, you know how you want things and when you want them. Loosen up!

The Ring Finger

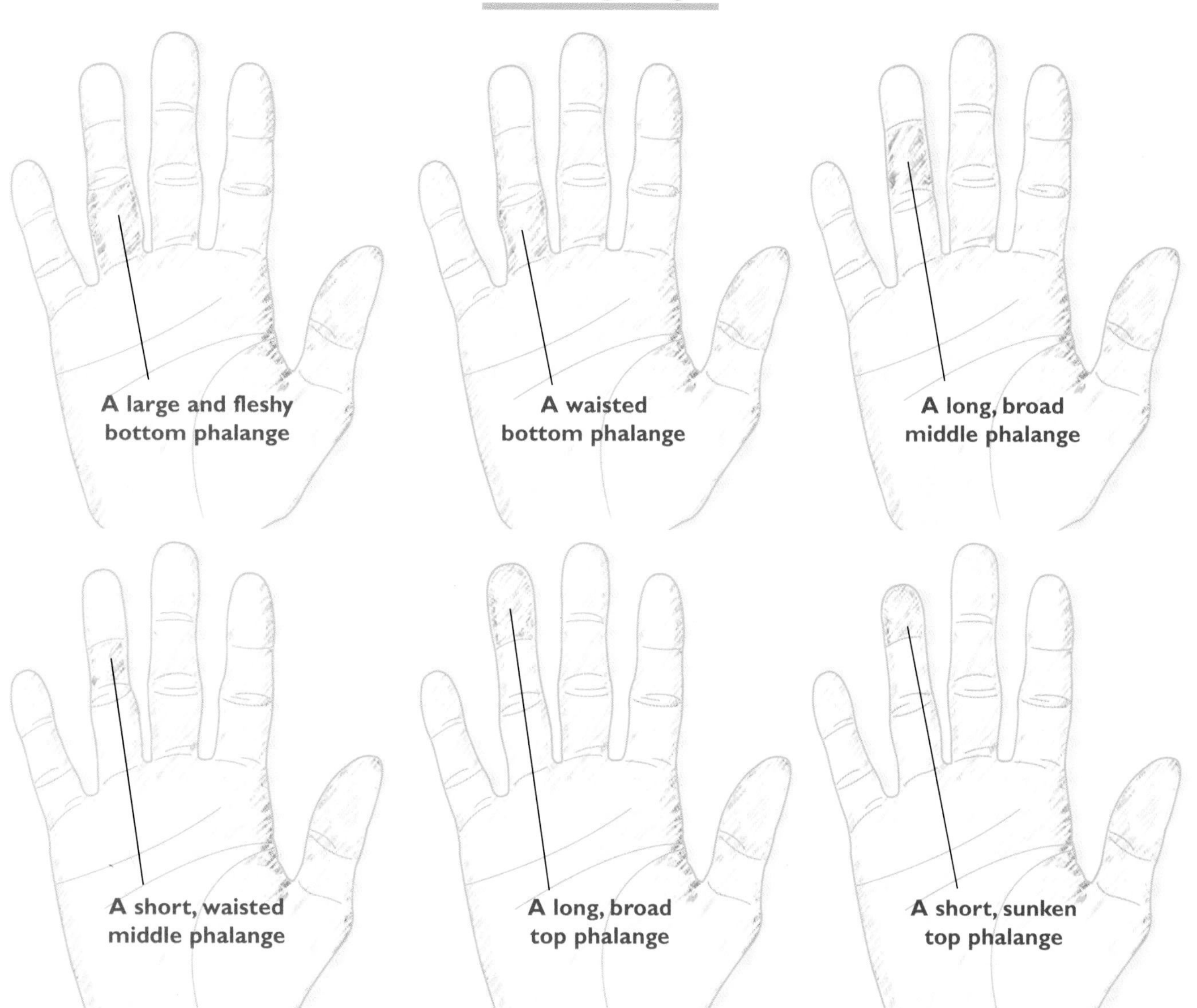

When the bottom phalange is large and fleshy. Feeling good and looking good are important to you. This is the sign of the decorator, cosmetologist, designer and artist. Comfort and class mean a lot. You like being in the company of creative people and are restless, curious about how others live.

When the bottom phalange is waisted. You may place more importance on other people than on yourself. You're good at comparison shopping, always on the lookout for bargains, and willing to make a sacrifice for what's fair and just. Learn to speak up for yourself. You probably know a little bit about many things and have a broad overview, but aren't proficient in any single area.

When the middle phalange is long, broad, or fleshy. You like leisurely recreation. Place a TV at the foot at your bed, or pipe in talk radio and dim the lights. You like being entertained by others, choosing to sit in the sidelines and watch.

When the middle phalange is short or waisted. Hobbies and personal pursuits are plentiful. You know how to entertain yourself and aren't concerned about next-door neighbors or world affairs.

When the top phalange is long, broad, or fleshy. You appreciate culture. You set high standards for yourself and expect others to do the same. You have a good eye for design, form, and color, and you appreciate all forms of beauty. Beware of prejudice and pettiness.

When the top phalange is short, sunken, or waisted. You may rely on the knowledge of others more than your own. Easily swayed by popular belief, it's important for you to develop your own set of standards.

The Little Finger

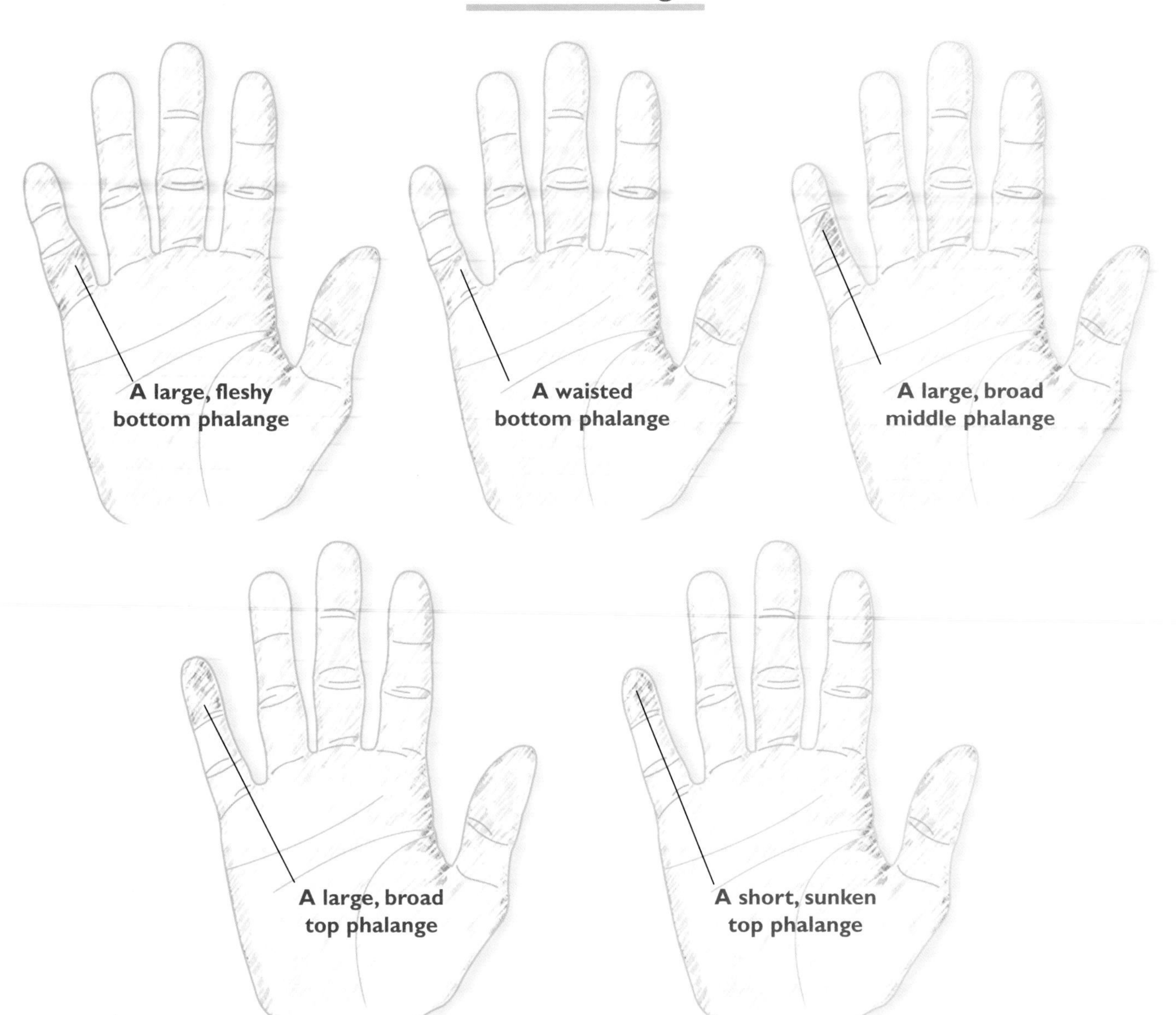

When the bottom phalange is large and fleshy. Your mind works in a logical and orderly way in obtaining financial or material security. If you can't touch it, it's not real. Sensual and physical, you like what money provides. Relationships may suffer due to overspending.

When the bottom phalange is waisted. You dream while others produce. You often say "I could've been a contender," and "If only I would've . . ." Don't put off until tomorrow what you can do now.

When the middle phalange is long, broad, or fleshy. You work until you get the job done. Able to make good use of your time, you're efficient and like working within well-established routines.

When the middle section is short or waisted but others are long, cooperation is needed. Insecure about your ability to do things on your own, you seek the approval of others. You don't like rocking the boat.

When the top phalange is long, broad, or fleshy. You have a powerful personal expression and belief in original ideas. You're seen by others as different or unusual. If there's a better way to do something, you'll discover it. You're a lover of efficiency and research.

When the top phalange is short, sunken, or waisted. You prefer the sidelines, doing things that are tried and true. The middle-of-the-road path is safest. Learning new formats is difficult. You like doing things like Momma or Daddy said and did.

The Thumb

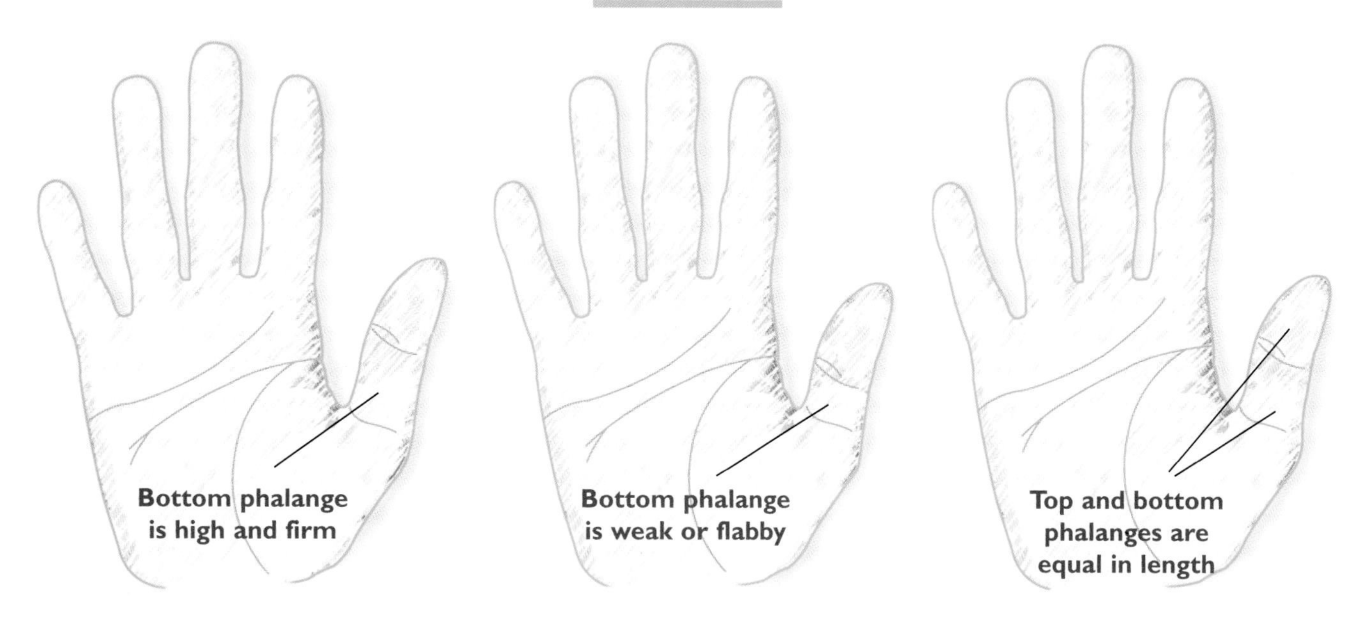

The thumb has only two phalanges—the top and the bottom.

When the thumb's bottom phalange is high and firm. You don't like others to hold you back. You're attracted to strong-willed people, confident go-getters. You are persistent, active, energetic, highly sensual. You work best alone, or when in command. You respond quickly to competition. You don't do well under restrictions because you like to make your own rules. You do what is asked and would thrive where you can be a teacher or leader.

You are generous, with a zest for life, and recover quickly and easily from illness. You're a rugged individual with an innate sense of drama. You enjoy personal attention, you're well-informed, and people seek out your conversation. Because you like people and have a talent for dealing with them, you might try a career in education, communications, or management.

When the bottom phalange is weak or flabby. You like being pampered. If you had it your way you probably wouldn't work at all! You prefer the "good life" and withdraw when the going gets rough. You probably have the talent for many things, but you need to "toughen up" to survive in the real, workaday world. Competition frightens or depresses you.

Mental stimulation comes from within your emotional core. You are inclined to think a great deal about ways to make yourself feel secure. Your cautious and meticulous nature enables you to excel at tasks that require attention to precision and detail. You get your kicks from being able to help others. Be careful not to neglect your own needs when others come looking for handouts or sympathy.

When the thumb's top and bottom phalanges are equal in length. You make decisions patiently and carefully, moderate in everything you do. You don't jump to conclusions, and you enjoy talking with others to find out what's on their mind. A natural diplomat, you discuss matters openly with coworkers and friends. You're not a "controller" and are tolerant of others' shortcomings. Jobs that allow some degree of authority and mobility suit you. You are good at planning and organizing. When others would explode or lose their temper, you keep your feelings under wraps.

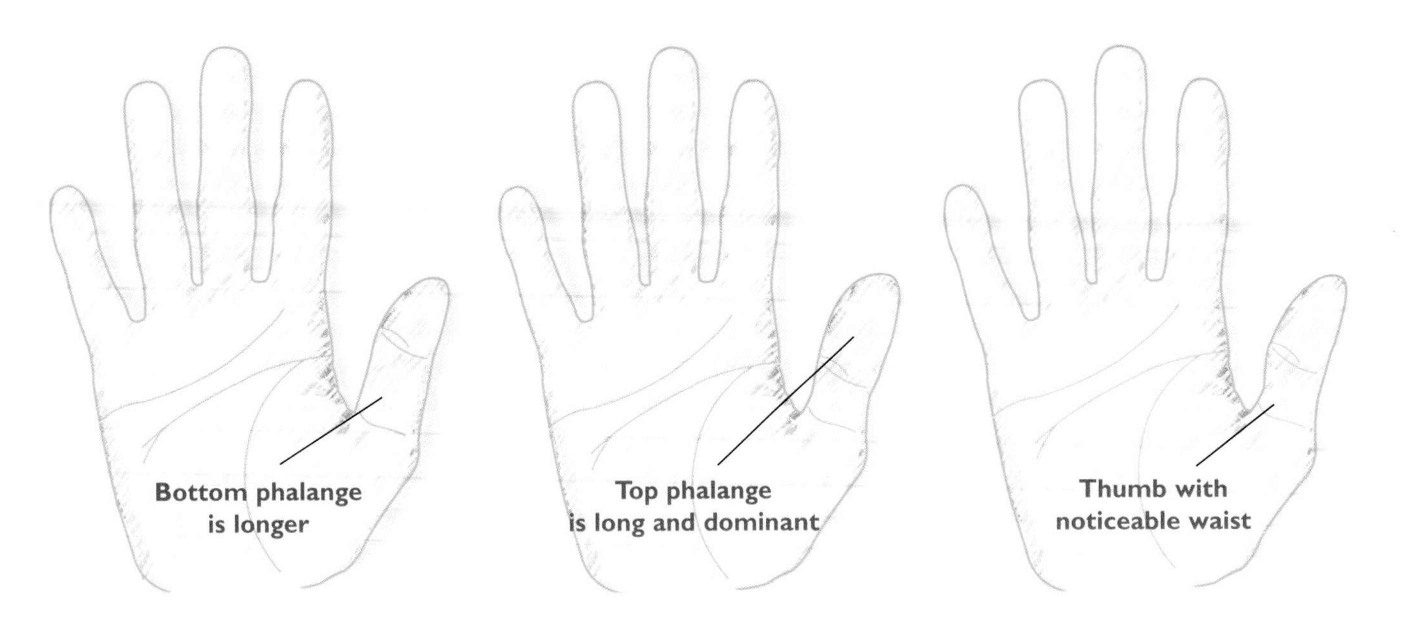

When the bottom phalange is longest. You don't mind working on your own provided it is on your terms. You're not comfortable dealing with unconventional or super-emotional people. You like having the final word but don't work well under pressure. You are well suited for jobs in which you use your mind and apply it directly to solve problems, such as technical occupations like science or mathematics.

When the top phalange is long and dominant. This suggests determination and a strong ego—your way! It's easy for you to break old habits and try new approaches. Routine bores you. It's not easy for you to follow someone else's orders unless it's someone you respect. Others may consider you obstinate because of your deep need to experience as much of life as possible. You enjoy being in the driver's seat—it's where you belong!

When the thumb has a noticeable waist. Tapering between the lower knuckle and the fleshy part of the palm reveals that you have boundless curiosity and a desire for self-improvement and to expand your horizons. You seek to rise above the monotony of daily life but are easily distracted, so you must discipline yourself to stay on course.

You have a talent for dealing with small groups and inspiring them to achieve excellence.

Fingertips

Fingertips come in five shapes, which are judged from the palm side of the hand rather than the back. Some hands have a mixture of finger shapes. Always note which shape is dominant. Generally, pointed tips are concerned with feelings; rounded, with others; squarish or blunt, with stability and business at hand.

Pointed Fingertips

These fingertips taper like a spade toward the end and reveal curiosity and a good imagination. A dreamy, sensitive escapist, you possess a rich fantasy life and enjoy being in love and nurturing others. You'd rather go along to get along. The ultimate peacemaker, your motto might be "Don't make waves."

Although not technically artistic, you appreciate music and the finer things of life. You have a wide range of interests and you understand the need to plan for your goals to achieve success. You find it essential to be loved and needed—by a partner, a plant, a child, or a Pekinese.

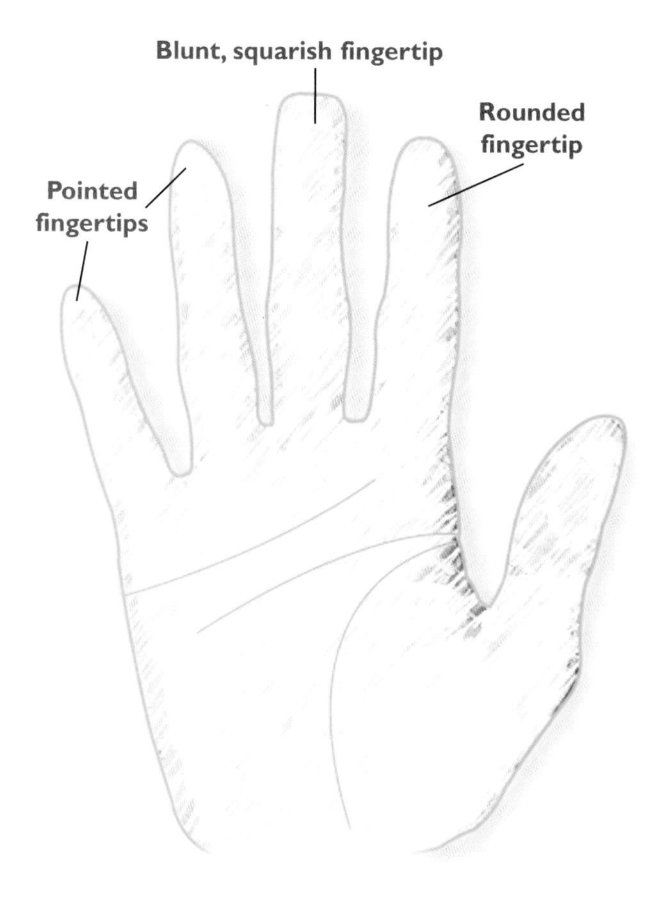

Rounded Fingertips

You enjoy people, are receptive, and react readily to outside stimuli. Rounded-fingertip types rarely like living alone. The constant presence of someone who cares for you makes your world safe and desirable. When you commit yourself in love, you do so totally and permanently. You are never pushy or forceful, but once you decide you want something you'll exert gentle but continuous effort to obtain it. You should consider careers that require helping others solve their problems: medicine, law, social work, or teaching.

Blunt, Squarish Fingertips

You gain emotional satisfaction from being careful, orderly, useful, and productive. Your self-reliance and stubborn determination make you great in the fields of sales and industry. You're a born manager, skilled at organizing others and delegating authority. You crave stability above all else, often viewing change as undesirable or threatening. You enjoy clearly defined gender roles, job descriptions, and deadlines.

Spatulate Fingertips

These flare at the tips and taper toward the knuckles, resembling a Japanese fan. People with spatulate fingertips love physical activity and the great outdoors. You enjoy a challenge and are excited by new conquests. You are vivacious, lively, and occasionally restless. You gain great satisfaction from doing, achieving, and making things—waiting around for slowpokes or listening to a long debate is not your cup of tea.

The ultimate individualist, you can't bear to have anyone else tell you what to do or how to do it, so you're a better solo act than a team player. If you can't do it on your own, you are at a loss. You have the drive and vitality to accomplish more than a dozen people. Those with spatulate fingertips don't mind when the going gets tough. You are hard-working and conscientious. You don't need feedback to assure you that you're on the right track—you prefer to work independently.

Bulbous Fingertips

This shape signifies a short temper. You rarely think about the consequences of your actions before you act and rarely let an obstacle stand in your way. You charge ahead, undaunted by risks. Try to look before you leap. Once you get going it's hard to keep up with you. Action is your middle name. Use compassion and consideration every now and then.

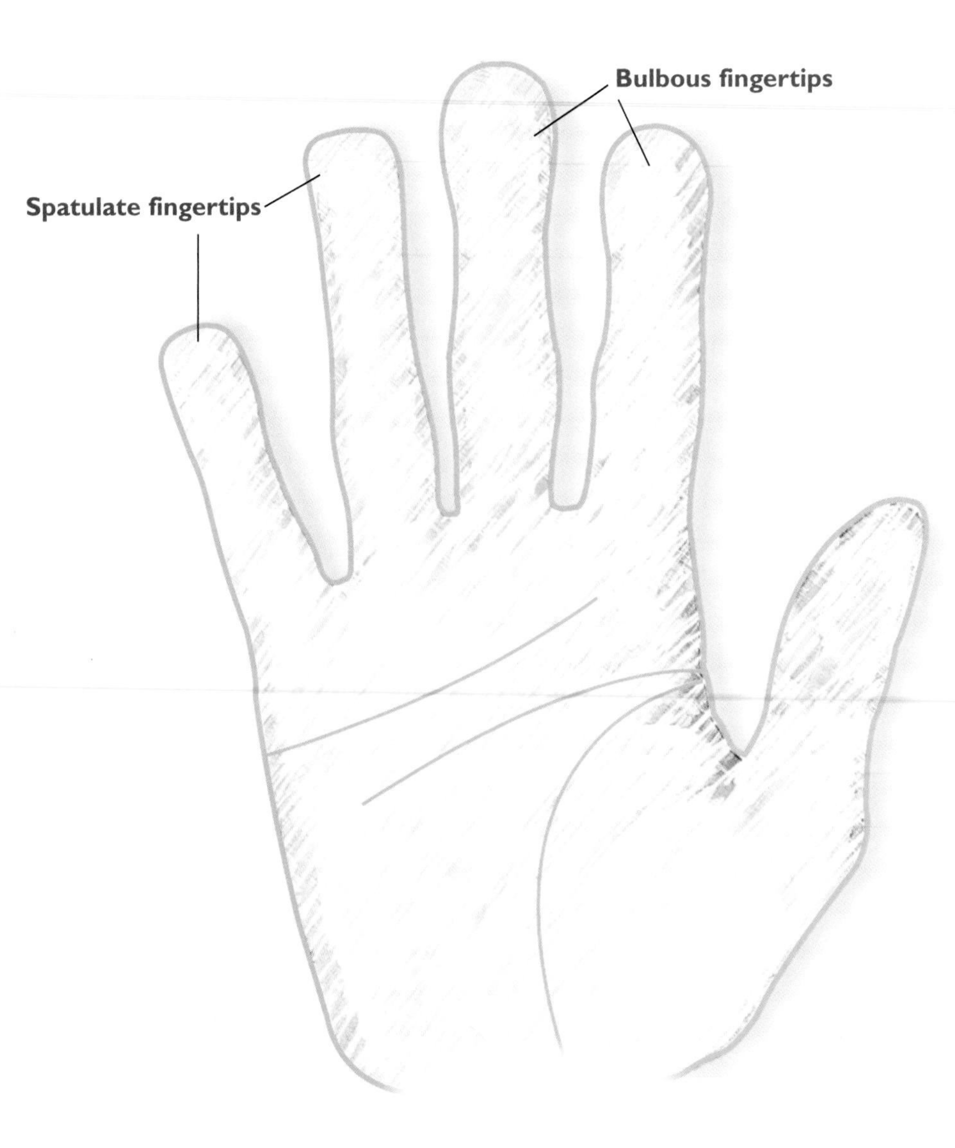

Fingernails

The study of fingernails took its place in the pantheon of human self-knowledge as *onyxology*, the Greek words for fingernail and speech. Just as a geologist looks at an ordinary rock and experiences thrilling revelations about the creation of this earth, an onyxologist can reveal a person's character, personality, and style of self-expression by scanning the texture, color, and shape of his fingernails.

Texture and Color

A healthy nail looks as smooth as glass and is pliable. It should have a visible semicircle, or half moon, at the nail bed. A half moon that's large suggests a heathy person. Half moons that shrink below the nail bed suggest a weaker constitution. Rough or brittle nails reveal anger, dissatisfaction, bitterness.

Rosy-pink nails reveal a strong, healthy physical disposition and a warm, positive approach to yourself and the world.

Rosy-red nails reveal a compulsive or impulsive nature with a will to win. You're reluctant to take orders and are aggressive, excitable, direct, and forceful. You can be hot-tempered and reckless.

Pale-white nails disclose low vitality, timidity, deference to others, and low self-esteem.

Yellowish nails indicate melancholy, helplessness, and despair. You need—but spurn—excitement. Unsympathetic and conceited, you can be quick to take offense or to blame others.

Grayish nails suggest someone who prefers not to get involved, a spectator in the game of life. Gray is often a prelude to blue.

Bluish nails are bad news. In addition to possibly having a circulatory disorder, you may be super-sensitive and confused, and have low self-esteem.

White spots (called *clouds*) most typically appear on children's fingernails. They appear wispy and feathery or thick and concentrated. They record periods of self-doubt and confusion. If they multiply and combine in layers, the person is experiencing enormous, persistent anguish and trouble. Allow about six months for clouds to grow upward and disappear. If clouds remain constant, suspect lack of self-love, feelings of inadequacy, and depression. Handle with care.

Spatulate Nails

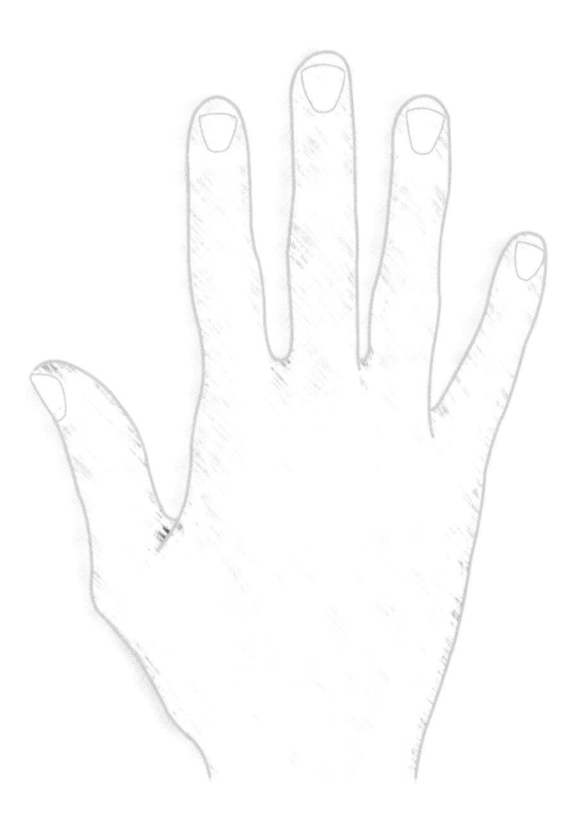

These look like a fan, a cone that's lost its ice cream, or a triangle standing on its point. You'll find spatulate nails on the hands of the go-getters. Active, unshockable, unpredictable, wonderfully inventive and resourceful, and always in a hurry, they are independent thinkers and a bit mischievous, living life to the fullest, showing affection easily. Good at making others happy, they are forever searching for new trails to blaze. They thrive on excitement and change, and find routine wretched.

On the index finger. You say what you feel and don't buy into criticism or "what you *should* do." Your glibness, self-confidence, and positive attitude make you the quintessential go-getting salesperson.

On the middle finger. You like to shock people and shake up institutions that have become too rigid. You are willing to stand up and fight for the rights of others and what you believe in.

On the ring finger. You approach everything with passion and intensity. You are the one called in to mediate family differences and squabbles at work. Be sure to make time for yourself.

On the little finger. You are insatiably curious and want to know and experience everything! Watch the bank balance, however, as accounting and budgets are not your forte.

On the thumb. You want things your way—period! Get the job done, get in, get out. You're a "bottom-liner" (and a bit grouchy).

Short, Squat Nails

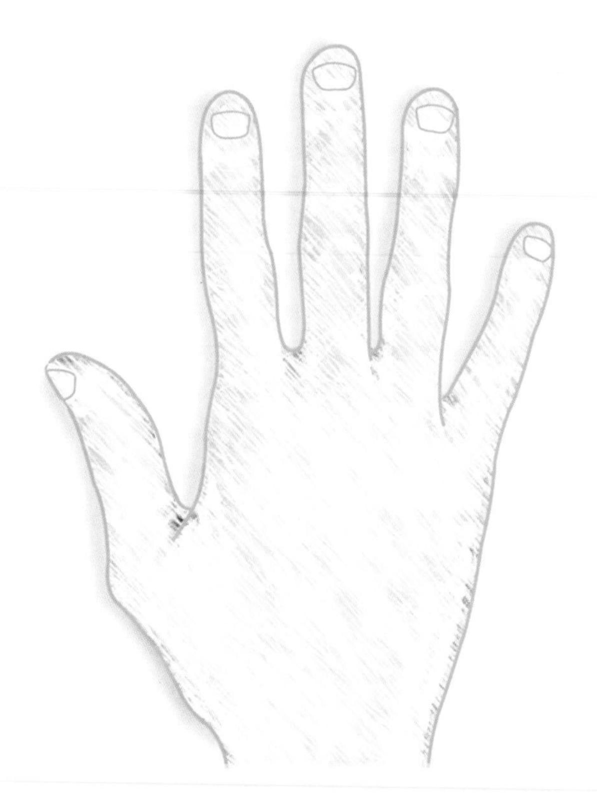

These look like a shoe box viewed sideways. These nails warn of stubborn, jealous, demanding, narrow-minded thinkers who don't like being wrong. Always on the defensive, you take yourself much too seriously for your own good. The shorter and wider the nail, the less on compassion for others. You pride yourself on effi-ciency and dedication to duty and can always be depended on to get the job done.

On the index finger. You need to guard against carrying perfectionism to extremes. You expect everyone around you to be perfect, but with impossibly high expectations, you often set yourself up for disappointment.

On the middle finger. Watch your temper! This is a sign of arrogance and irritability. You tend to find security, stability, and protection in external things but may forget emotiona nurturing. When things don't work as planned loosen up!

On the ring finger. You don't like being, working, or living alone. Whether from coworkers, friends, or family, it's important to have a steady support system for acknowledgment. You hate spreading yourself too thin.

On the little finger. You are reluctant to try anything new and are anything but adventurous. You don't place much weight on abstractions or happenstance. You enjoy control, owning the maestro's baton, and embellishing everything you do with your personal touch.

On the thumb. Aim for compromise, not confrontation. Emotions are too unpredictable and messy. You're a facts-first, just-do-your-job person.

Square Nails

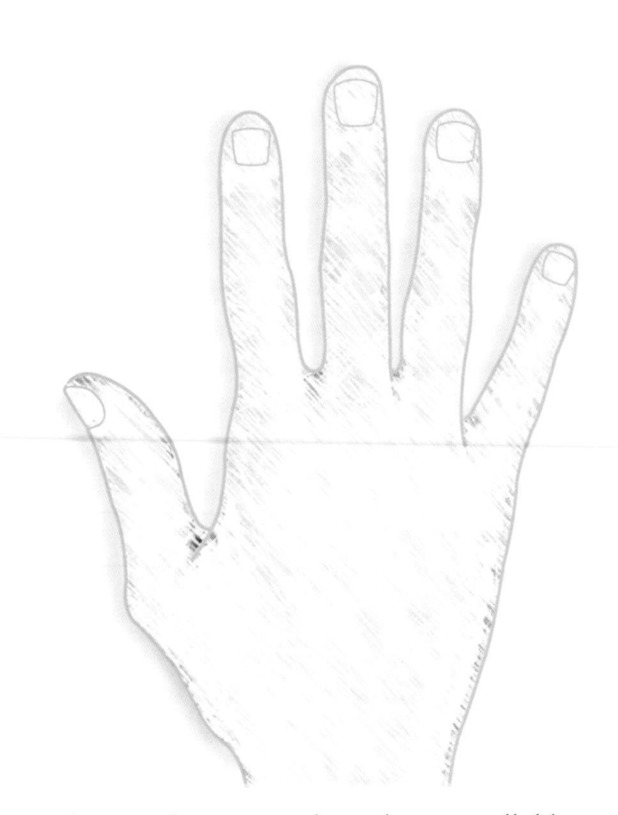

These nails are as wide as they are tall, like a child's building block. You're the Rock of Gibraltar: steady, secure, straightforward. You're slow to anger, take great pains to express your intentions thoughtfully and clearly, and are to the point in matters of love. You're honest, economy-conscious and dependable, leaving the details to others. You're an efficient manager and administrator.

On the index finger. You're put off by dishonesty and insincerity and are critical of shoddy workmanship. You roll up your sleeves and pitch in at the eleventh hour—and expect others to do the same. You enjoy being seen as dependable and enjoy a reputation of being trustworthy and organized.

On the middle finger. You have a conservative nature. You don't rock the boat of popular thinking. You dislike being questioned and enjoy getting your money's worth. You expect those around you to pitch in and do their share.

On the ring finger. You're adaptable and practical, with a good head for business. Organized and efficient, you work well with others and don't let anyone push you around. Everything you do, you give it your all.

On the thumb. You are happiest when busy; you work hard and expect the same from others. You treasure tradition and structured approaches to life. You hate to be caught short when deadlines approach. Like the tortoise, you win the race slowly but surely.

Oval Nails

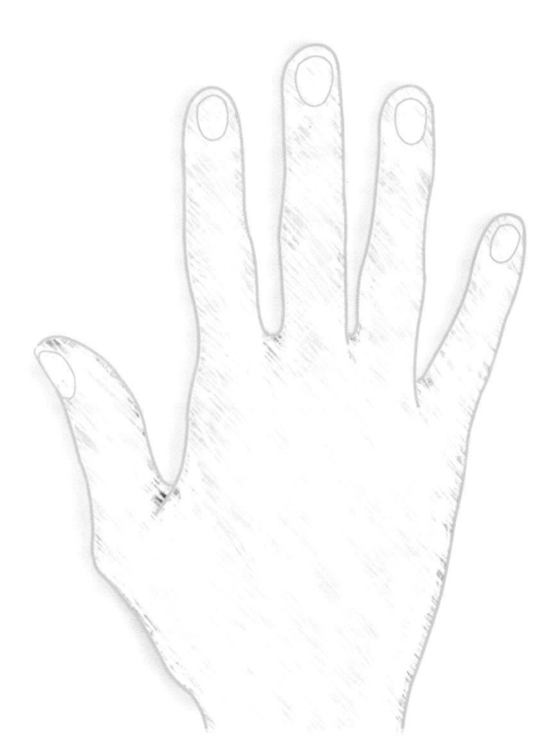

Oval nails reveal one who is flexible, open-minded, adaptable. You can make a home out of a room at the Holiday Inn! You're idealistic, imaginative, expressive, genuinely concerned for others, and always there when needed. You're also sociable and dreamy; "Your place or mine?"

On the index finger. You can't bear conflict or hostility of any kind, nor can you stand to have anyone mad at you. You aim to make a good impression and to have everyone like you. You're strong at maintaining balance and harmony at all times.

On the middle finger. You're a planner, negotiator, and peacemaker. You aim for middle-of-the-road agreements, not wanting to make waves. Because you may lack perseverance, you work best on a team.

On the ring finger. You are an agreeable, rational individual and master strategist. You're good at laying out plans for others, and you objectively analyze every situation.

On the little finger. You're generally easy-going and good-natured, rarely staying angry for long. You say what you feel while always embracing the status quo. You don't like rocking the boat. Have faith in your own opinions.

On the thumb. You have trouble setting limits for yourself. You make friends easily; profit-making and personal gratification are rarely a priority. Learn to use your communication skills effectively and forcefully. Look out for Number One.

Almond-Shaped Nails

You are unassuming, refined, and friendly, with a knack for seeing both sides of a problem. Intellectually zealous, you strive for precision and perfection, with an eye for beauty, dignity and balance.

On the index finger. You like peace, at any cost—especially when your name is associated with the terms. You can't stand for anyone to dislike you. Concerned with your reputation, you make sure any job with your name on it is done properly. Though politeness is your policy, you are compelled to ask questions.

On the middle finger. You're good at analyzing character and what makes people tick. You're more curious than quick and have a reputation

Almond-shaped nails

Rectangular nails

Datestone nails

for keeping your word. Still, you're fussy about your choice of friends and enjoy your own good company while observing from the sidelines.

On the little finger. You have a deep need to be loved. You feel empty when there's no significant other in your life. Loyal and caring, you crave unions and companionship. You're a soft-hearted romantic.

On the thumb. You are forthright and honest in your dealings with others. "Peace at any price" is your motto. You'll do anything in the name of love or compromise. You genuinely enjoy people and include a wide variety of acquaintances within your circle. Be selective. You deserve it!

Rectangular Nails

These nails are long with squared-off bases, resembling a shoe box viewed upright. These folks learn by doing, not by study. They relate with feelings and passionate, sentimental (sexual) emotions, not with the harsh, cold intellect. The longer the nail shape, the deeper your feelings run true and the more compassion you exhibit.

On the index finger. You present a pleasant, friendly face to the world. You are gracious and know how to meet the public. You encourage others to come to you for answers and would do well as a teacher, office organizer, or therapist.

On the middle finger. You like to be in charge but are soft-hearted. You don't mean to hurt anyone, but you need the freedom to pursue your own interests. Proud of your effect on others, you enjoy adulation.

On the ring finger. You desire to keep everybody happy. Service to others gives you pleasure, and you are generous with your advice. But even though you cherish peace and harmony, you would sooner rock the boat than shirk your responsibility.

On the little finger. Variety is your greatest need. Freedom to travel makes you happy. Never at a loss for words, you need to be seen as well as heard—always part of what's happening.

On the thumb. Aim for discretion. You're a pushover. You tend to take more than your share of guff and go to great lengths to avoid unpleasant confrontations. Your goal is to play by the rules of integrity and justice. Don't lose sight of yourself or your own needs.

Datestone Nails

These nails are thinner than rectangular nails. These folks can be critical and high-strung. They tend to nag and pick, and they rarely have anything nice to say. They overreact to the slightest demands of family and coworkers. On any finger, this nail shape suggests narrow-mindedness.

Fingerprints

Your fingerprints are your unique credentials, distinguishing you from all others, unchanging throughout your lifetime. There are three basic designs. Each hand may carry more than one pattern. Examine your hand and note the dominant pattern. Some fingers may carry composite prints—a blend of two or more patterns. In such cases, note the dominant image.

The Loop

The most frequent fingerprint pattern seen, the loop resembles a cowboy's lasso. If you have a majority of loops, you're adaptable, agreeable, and unlikely to rock the social boat. You thrive on social interaction and maintain a large circle of acquaintances whom you speak with frequently—even with those who live far away. You're a sentimentalist at heart.

You make the most of every situation and truly care about what others think. You have difficulty expressing true feelings or opinions sometimes. Sympathetic to the needs of others, you are always willing to pitch in and lend a helping hand. On the work front you are at your best when projects are clearly defined and laid out, because you tend to drift aimlessly and go in circles. You perform well whenever emergencies arise and are quick on your feet. You have a lightning-fast wit, are inventive, and enthusiastic.

On the index finger. You can improvise and act in many capacities. You are a friendly person who is easy to get along with and are willing to laugh at yourself. You can see your way around obstacles and are versatile in your thinking. One weak point may be an inclination to start several projects at once. Your mind is quick but your staying power is short, leaving the impression that you are more idealistic than practical.

On the middle finger. You are fond of intellectual discussions and eager to learn more. You challenge and ask questions until you feel that you have a clear understanding of others' statements, but you always take care not to violate anyone's privacy. You are deeply inquisitive. You have a good talent for organization because you pay attention to small details (especially, if you have long fingers) while always keeping the overall objective in mind. You are a person who likes to make the most use of available time. If the loop pattern is low on your finger, there may be an attraction in forestry, farming, gardening, or ecological pursuits.

On the ring finger. You are sociable. Your associates often find your conversations inspiring and contagious because of your wonderful way with words. You treat others fairly and with respect, and are willing to negotiate, to go that extra mile. You set high standards of behavior for yourself as well as your coworkers and are always open to constructive criticism. Honesty, for you, is the best policy.

On the little finger. You have the unique ability to discover hidden evidence below the surface and are determined to make your ideals real. You dislike being tied down and should seek tasks that allow you a degree of freedom. Your shrewd, creative mind enables you to produce good works of imagination. You spurn attachments to material things and make few demands on the time and attention of friends.

You are broad-minded, fair, and polite, but you're inclined to take sides with the weak or the underdog. You're open to new suggestions and very flexible with other points of view. Others admire your integrity and ethics, and you stick to your guns when you know you are right. Your greatest gift is the talent to see ideas and to make them work for improving a situation. With your tendency to overwork, it's important that you get enough sleep and eat healthfully.

On the thumb. You have a strong stamina. You are able to stick to schedules imposed by others and you respect rules and standard procedures. You are the type who strives to be everything to everyone, no holding back. Disinclined to pass unfair judgments, it is easy for you to warm up to strangers. You are affectionate and sociable and can usually be relied upon to keep your word. You will shine in any career you choose because you are prepared to pay the piper full price for success.

The Arch

This fingerprint looks like an upside-down T and is commonly found on the fingers of efficient, hard-working, and reliable people. Your mind works in an orderly and organized fashion. You take nothing at face value, dissecting everything to see what makes it tick. You have a good memory for facts, figures, and words. Your keen analytical ability makes you ideal for fields like repair, accounting, book editing, computer programming, and research. Cautious and conservative, you tend to be more of a follower than an intellectual pioneer.

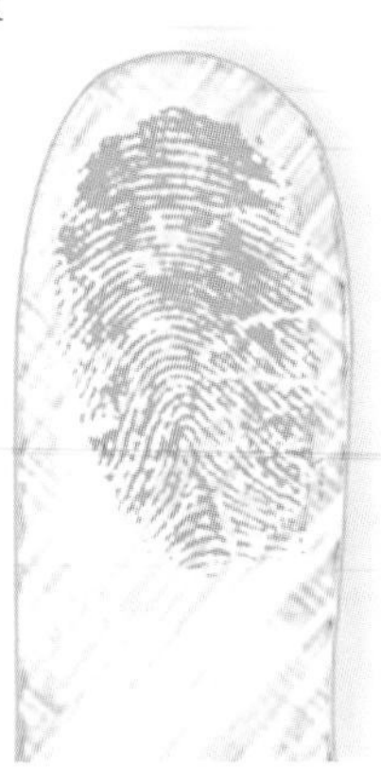

Are most of your prints arches? If so, you won't accept the values or proposals of others without careful consideration and discernment. When deadlines near, you work hard, cover all bases, and see things through to the end.

On the index finger. You are more comfortable working with what's tried and true rather than speculative or undefined. In a world where appearances count, friends and coworkers view you as reliable, solid, and dependable. Instead of forcing a situation to materialize, you plot, plan and persevere until you devise a winning strategy. Your personal aims are never too far out of sight because the goals you set are realistic and exact.

Getting involved in idle gossip doesn't cut the cake. For you work should be work, and your personal life is separate. On the job, you are inclined to be conscientious to a fault, so it is important that you learn to relax and not get too down on yourself. You enjoy sensible efficiency and seldom lift your nose from the grindstone until you punch out.

On the middle finger. You attach yourself to things that grow in value—friendships maintained for years, investments that compound daily. Your keywords are reliability and substance. Fads hold little interest for you. You seek to uncover the truths behind matters and are fascinated by world governments, multinational corporations, and enduring traditions. You are a patient, plodding individual who goes through life not expecting instant results, feedback, or constant praise. You feel all efforts you make will eventually be rewarded.

You eliminate without hesitation people and problems you consider useless or inappropriate. Many see you as a loner or a person of inflexible action. You are discreet and business-minded, always on the lookout for substantial ways to make money from your and other people's talents. Research work, antiques, precious gems, and jobs that require facts or theories would be rewarding. You are discriminating, dependable, thorough, and precise, and need an outlet for these constructive characteristics.

On the ring finger. You have a "be here now" attitude, and you're an honest, outspoken person. You have a good eye for detail, particularly if your fingers are long. Perfection is your goal, and you possess a sharp, discriminating sense. You enjoy working with structured aims so that your time is used competently and efficiently. You are sure to find success provided you are not pushed too fast, and you can work alone.

You are attracted to jobs that require a talent for coordinating form or color, neatness, or organization. You must find a measure of peace and harmony in your vocation and your working environment.

On the little finger. You represent a scant one percent of people worldwide. If you carry this rare print, you are inclined to need strong people to lean on. You love to be complimented, cuddled and needed. You are extremely compassionate in colleague's sorrows but may tend to be possessive and overprotective of everyone but yourself. You can never get enough reassurance that you are well-liked or respected, so you have a tendency to involve yourself in everyone else's crises to feed the need to be important.

You have a good head for facts and figures—especially when they have nothing to do with you. Helping others makes you feel better about yourself. Occupations such as medicine, counseling, and ghosting behind (rather than in) the spotlight could provide a quirky kind of happiness. The desire to promote an ideal is strong.

You are forthright and honest in your dealings with others and incredibly sincere.

On the thumb. You have very little interest in abstract thought or theories. Facts and the why-and-wherefore of things are your primary drive. You make up your mind quickly as an efficient, loyal, and thoughtful person. You are a good listener and can identify easily with the plight and sorrow of others, expecting little in return. With your noble principles, you will give a lifetime of dedication once you discover a cause worthy of this devotion.

No matter what work you choose, others will look to you for guidance. Whatever you undertake you do patiently and with thoroughness. You are not afraid of responsibility. You have a cool steadiness and strong shoulders to lean on for others weaker than yourself. Your honesty and dependability will bring you many rewards at work and much satisfaction from employers and family.

The Whorl

This fingerprint looks like the bull's eye and is the sign of an individualist. Self-expression is important, and you especially enjoy exploring new ideas and concepts. Conventional wisdom and accepted truths don't hold much in your book—you're eager to contest them with original ideas of your own. Even when your ideas and dreams are grandiose or unrealistic, you never believe they're impossible. Something of a flatterer, you're charming and very interested in romance.

You're slow to make up your mind about matters, always trying to see what tomorrow holds. You are comfortable when sharing the company of artistic or adventurous souls and are eager for applause. Your professional affairs benefit from your innate ability to detect dishonesty and deception, so careers requiring investigation, diplomacy and trustworthiness would be best. Sensitive, independent, spontaneous, and personable describe the characteristics of those with whorl fingerprints.

Are all your prints whorl-shaped? If so, you are best described as zany, eccentric, and fast-moving. You are gregarious to a fault, with a tendency to go overboard every time. You possess keen sensitivity, deep emotions, and an extremely well developed imagination. Although your intentions are basically good and honorable, you have a closely guarded aura of secrecy you only let down with a chosen few. You could be a charismatic actor or actress, an inspiring writer, an astute astrologer or psychic, or an artist. One thing's for sure: you don't want to be overlooked!

On the index finger. You choose to do things your way; activities that are repetitious and routine spell instant boredom for you. You act on your own beliefs and prefer a career that provides you great independence, activity, and personal contact. In no time at all you can take the most boring, superficial job and create a special niche that makes you indispensable.

A little flattery gets you most places, doesn't it? You enjoy feeling important, and you take pride in all of your accomplishments. You display constant optimism and warmth, and associates regard your opinions as trustworthy and noble, but at times eccentric. Look for jobs in which you can demonstrate yourself. Careers in public life, entertainment, parapsychology, personnel, and health are well suited to you. Whatever you choose, you'll take the spotlight and climb to the top in no time!

On the middle finger. You're a quick learner and an industrious self-starter. Your organizational skills are acute, and you have a good sense of justice and fair play. You handle difficult situations without too much worry and can get things done with a minimum of fuss or bother. Friends and coworkers see you as an opinionated and strongly principled person who sticks to his or her guns.

Organizing and delegating a place for everything is one of your strengths. You realize your own level of competence and are good at figuring out and assessing others. You need a working life that is meticulous, neat, and orderly because you are exacting, clinical, and contemptuous of distraction. Whatever goal you aim for, you're always precisely on-target.

On the ring finger. You have the ability to take the disconnected ideas of others and turn them into realistic and sensible plans. You are

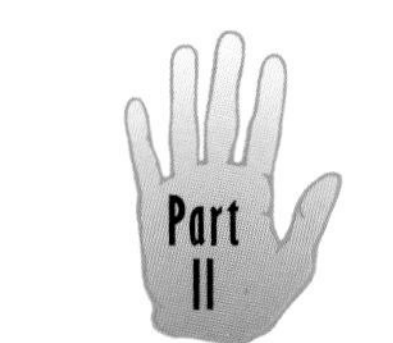

optimistic about yourself and skillful at expressing your needs. You are best suited to jobs in which you are free to draw your own conclusions, because discovery and creativity provide much pleasure to you. This print is good for jobs that require originality or alternative pathways. You are able to grasp ideas and beliefs that others miss.

You are impatient with repetition and rigid ways and have no patience for drone work. Your clothes and home decor all carry your distinctive tattoo. Your philosophy of life is progressive and artsy, and you are highly aware of who you are and where you want to go. You could achieve success in any spot that requires balance, ingenuity, design, or artistic impression.

On the little finger. You want life to flow smoothly because you're not the aggressive type. Whenever trouble begins to brew, you're always willing to lend a hand in settling the conflict. You get along well with others and inspire a sense of calm and harmony. You are more willing than most to compromise, because being on good terms with others is important to you.

You adapt at making conciliatory deals and can be a hard task master whenever you are in a position of power. Normally you are quiet and efficient, working your way up to the top with calculated, well-thought-out plans. Reliable and steady, you let everyone around you know what you feel, both positive and negative. You are fastidious about your professional appearance and do not give in to unjust criticism. You are progress-oriented and probably have an excellent record of reliability and stamina.

On the thumb. You have inexhaustible energy. Almost everything you do stems from imagination, inspiration, or impulse. You are vital and extremely clever, winning over associates with your infectious manner. You carry on conversations with almost anyone because you are a good listener and speaker.

You are always careful not to offend or invalidate others and usually let people think whatever they choose—provided that they leave you and your ideas intact. You enjoy gossip and hearing of the misfortunes of others. You enjoy being the first and the best, so assuming authority comes naturally. Although you are confident that you can handle anything that arises, you are really more of a "mental" rather than "physical" type of person—mind over muscle—so always be on guard against carelessness and accidents.

Part III
The Palm

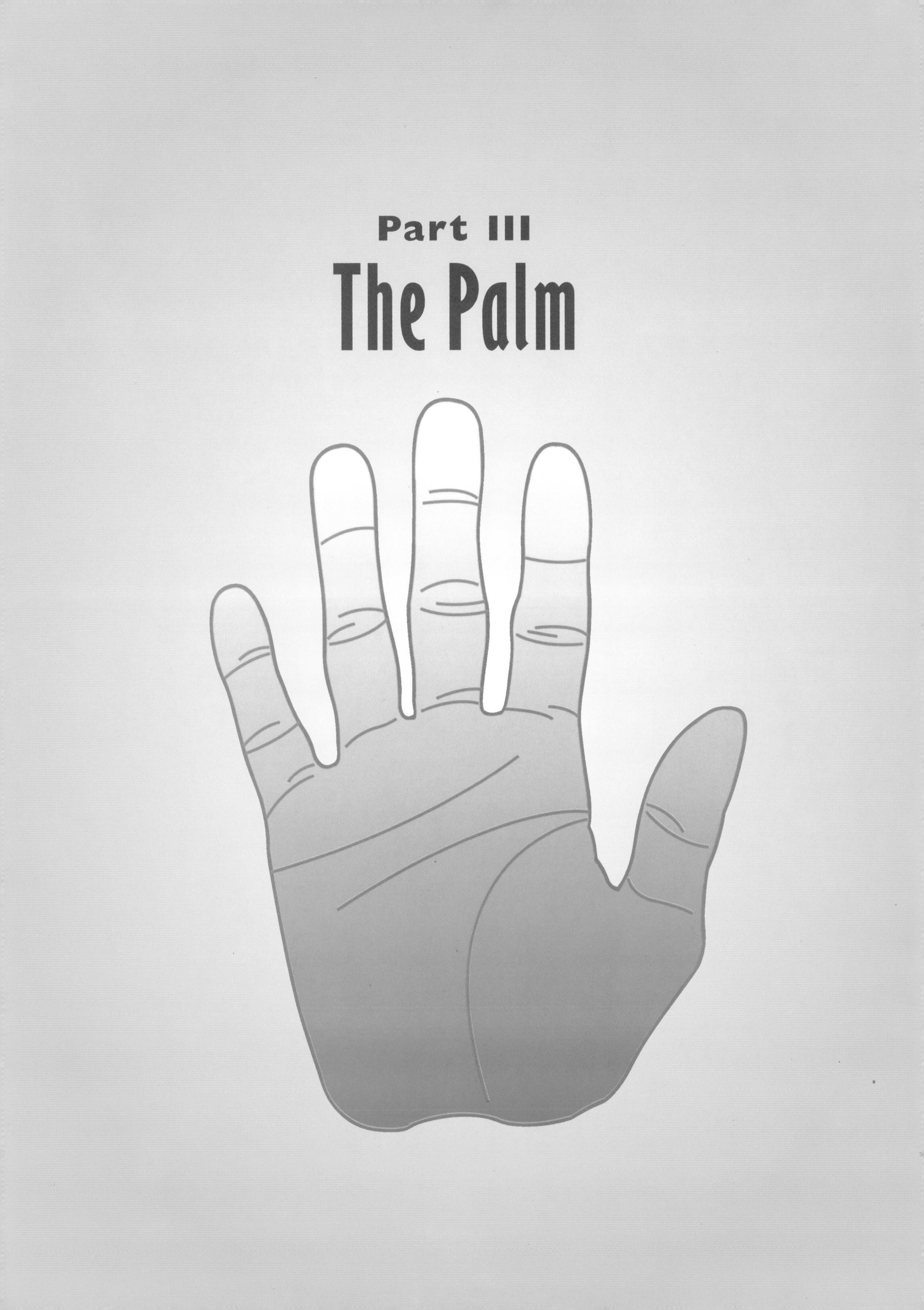

Major Lines

There are a few guidelines for looking at palm lines. In general, the more lines, the more emotional you are. Palms with very few lines tell of a more physical, practical, organized spirit. Fine, thin lines signal someone who is more intellectual and creative. An excess of fine lines suggests nervous and scattered energy. Deep, wide lines mark someone with strong opinions. Chained, feathery or broken lines suggest someone who has fragile self-esteem. Breaks suggest diminishing energy of the line's character. Forks suggest options.

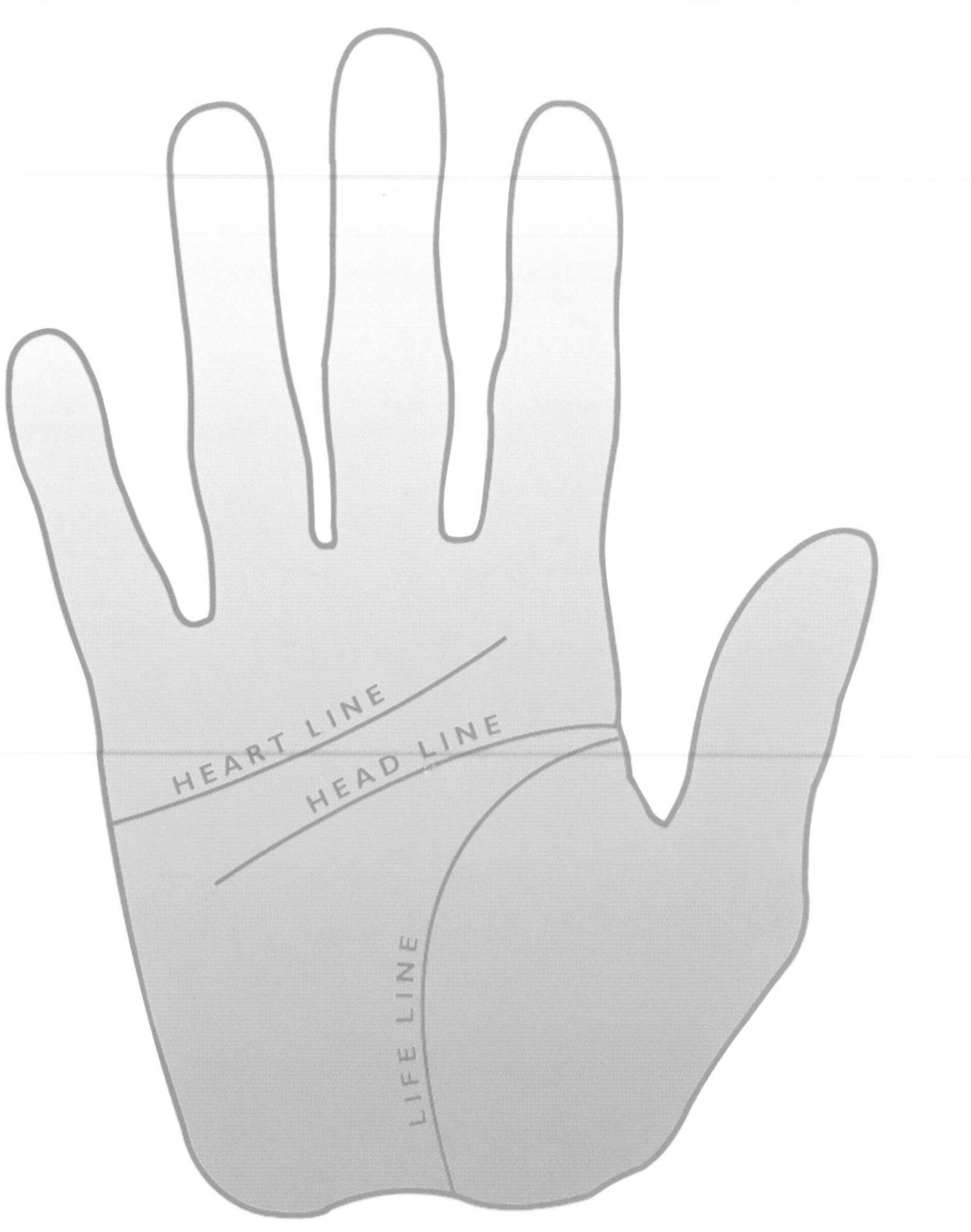

The Life Line

Also called the Vitality Line, the Life Line doesn't reveal how long you'll live, but rather speaks of your enthusiasm for living and willingness to fight for what you want and love. It embraces the elevated area beneath the thumb called the Mount of the Sun—the life-giver.

When the Life Line is deeply etched, free of breaks and tassels. This assures a robust and fruitful life. You are a high-energy person who embraces opportunity and challenge. Affectionate and physically demonstrative, you enjoy life and people. You're known for your courage, energy, and desire to win. You don't let problems or disappointments get you down for long, quickly putting failures behind you so you can begin your next adventure. You're eager to learn everything you can, preferably through personal experience. Your curiosity is boundless.

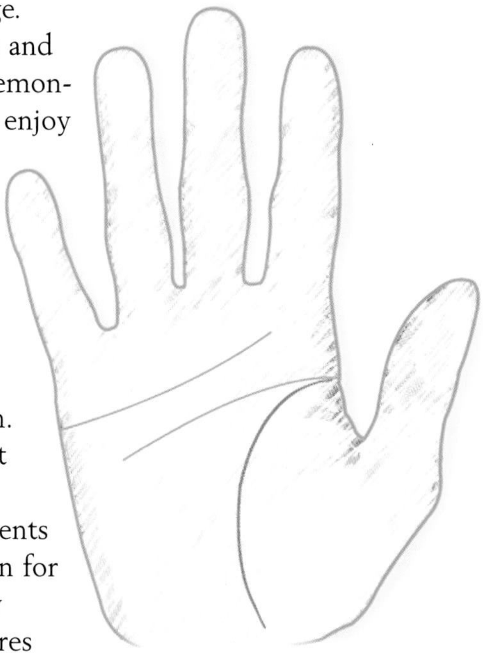

When it breaks up or disappears, or is faintly etched. You probably spend more time thinking than taking action. You owe it to yourself to be more assertive. You sometimes try to avoid reality through escapism and may be unwilling to take on such responsibilities as emotional commitments, earning a living, and paying your bills. You may feel your role is more one of helping others lead, but you must learn to assert your own ideas, too. Don't be fearful of taking charge. Traditional values and structures that have survived the test of time appeal to you most. You are the loyal, conscientious good citizen. You believe all people are created equal and should have the same rights and freedoms. You'd be a great juror, social worker, or teacher of the physically or mentally challenged.

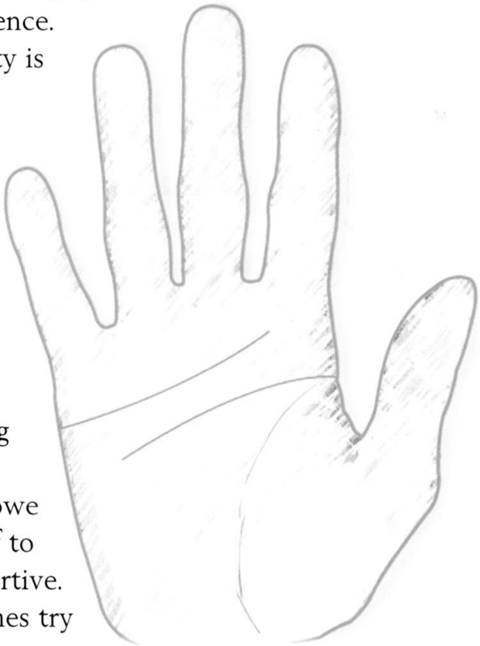

When it makes a wide, sweeping curve across the palm. You're a magnanimous, sunny individual, generous to a fault. You can bring a breath of fresh air into stale situations. Although you're always looking to the future, you never risk losing touch with the present or not learning from the past. At your best, you're always looking for new options and experiences, your style tends to be assertive and energetic.

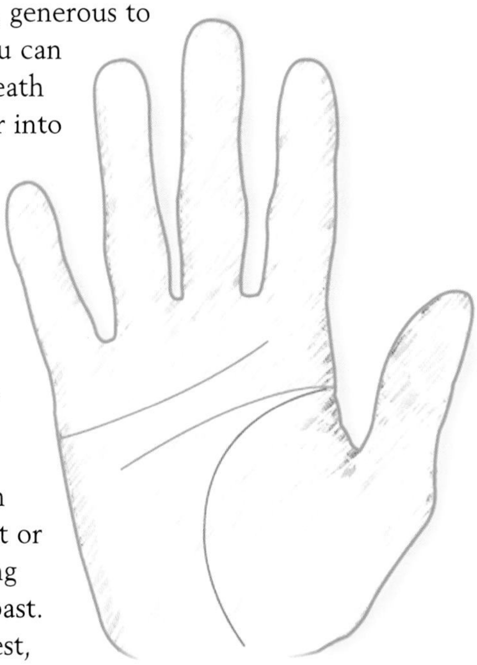

At your worst, you may seek change for the sake of change; always remember to consider alternatives to replace the structures you want to improve. You enjoy being seen as strong and reliable, respected, and loved. You give freely of your time and money. You enjoy each day and want to explore new horizons. If things stay calm for too long you become bored. You bounce back quickly from disappointments, eager to move on.

When it starts high up on or very near the base of the index finger. You're an ambitious, risk-taking person. You expand your understanding of the world at large by taking chances and pushing the envelope. You test your own limits and those of others around you. You never know what you can do until you try, try again . . . and again.

Because you idealize independence and individuality, you may resent having to play by the rules, and you are not especially interested in being accepted by any group. You have a strong dramatic sense and can be plenty flamboyant in the way you go about expressing yourself. You believe your rightful place is Number One. Never forget that the king depends on his subjects as much as they rely on him.

When it hugs the thumb closely. You may shy away from the spotlight. Your passions rarely rule your thinking and you rarely act in anger. Though you are not naturally a fighter, you are a mother lion when it comes to protecting friends, family, and home. You enjoy helping others and constantly think about their greater good. You like your environment to be balanced and congenial, choosing to unite with others instead of opposing them. Concerned with justice and fairness, you don't let your ego get in the way of actions or decisions. Although you may not be willing to stand up for yourself, you won't be pushed around.

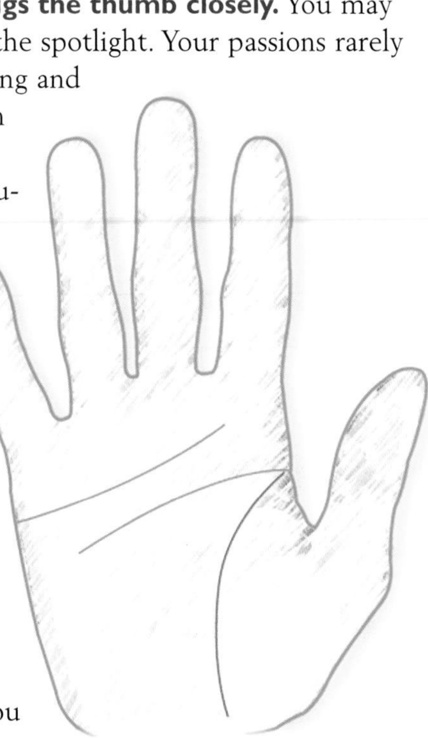

You don't like competition or antagonism. You prefer to make friends, not adversaries. You're a bit private and inclined to withdraw. Get plenty of sleep, because you could be hyperactive or prone to allergies. Try boosting your stamina with regular exercise and by eating well.

When it's doubled. Two or three concentric lines instead of one warns you to look before you leap! Impulsive and overly confident, you love challenges, even conflict, and you may be a bit accident-prone. Once you get going, it's hard to keep up with you. Aim to develop your attention span. You lose interest quickly, always ready to try something more exciting or new. You have an innate sense of the dramatic and always do things with a flair. Flattery feeds your sizable ego (and you like nothing better). Nothing hurts you more than being unappreciated. You have trouble seeing your friends and family as individuals, and you need to guard against thinking of them as mere extensions of yourself.

Establishing financial security for your later years will help you maintain a plan of action and see it realized. Invest in a partnership to give you the initiative to accomplish more than you otherwise might. Develop goals that are within your reach and work diligently toward them. You'll achieve the long-lasting security you want if you plan realistically and work for it.

When it's straight and short. Your deepest, most fundamental need is to be free. Short, straight Life Lines that stop abruptly suggest restlessness. Your love relationships are probably more romantic friendships than hot, passionate affairs. As an idealist, you usually believe that things will always turn out for the best. Even when you stumble, you pick yourself up and bounce back from defeat. However, you need physical outlets for your restlessness. Try anything—walking, raking leaves, or swimming. Don't wait for the "perfect" moment to begin; start now.

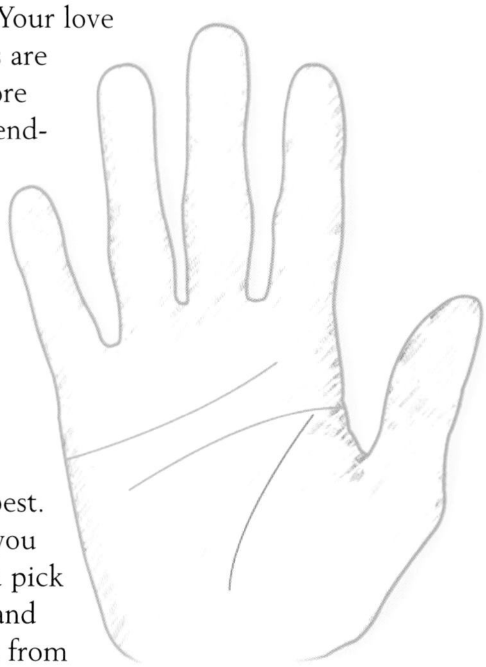

You know better than anyone else that you must plan ahead if you want success. You like to pamper yourself and may have a hard time keeping your finances in order; you tend to spend money as soon as you get it. Stop wasting resources and creative talents and be more realistic about achieving freedom from financial anxiety.

When it's broken or separated. Despite honorable intentions, you usually fail to finish what you start, scattering yourself with trivial pursuits. Although open-minded, you tend to overestimate yourself or don't plan ahead wisely. You rarely look back, so you don't learn from your mistakes. Refrain from climbing out on limbs that lead nowhere and stop overestimating yourself and others. Don't let your imagination run away with you. Gentle, sympathetic, and idealistic, you are easily fooled and can be taken in by unscrupulous people. Let common sense be your guide.

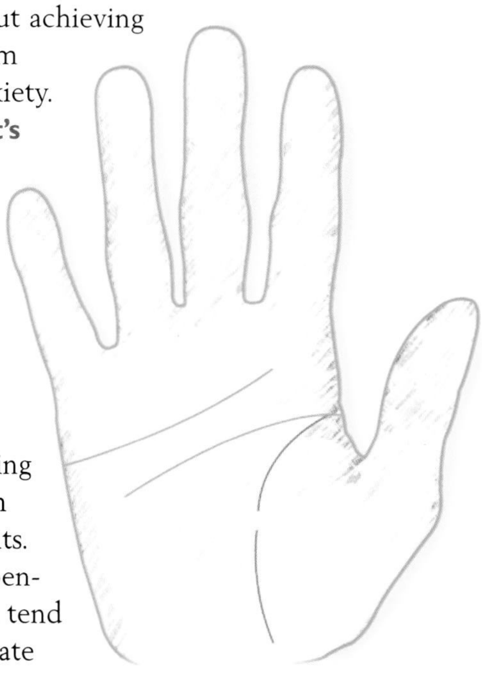

Don't be envious of others because you assume they are more resourceful than you, for that may not be the real deal. You're too easily intimidated by competition, so you don't assert yourself often enough. Making the right decisions for yourself, in spite of your family's or colleague's opinions, is a critical factor for your future success. With your wealth of ideas, there are unlimited ways you can apply your skills to achieve goals and gain the security you crave.

When it's composed of a series of breaks or "chains." You tend toward escapism. You're susceptible to hard-luck stories and have a problem with priorities. Your opinions are often based on hazy impressions or romantic notions. Your heart is touched by sob stories of those worse off than you, and you may find yourself continually involved with dependent friends and lovers, sacrificing your desires for them. You're basically a private person, inclined to withdraw from worldly activities. You require plenty of sleep.

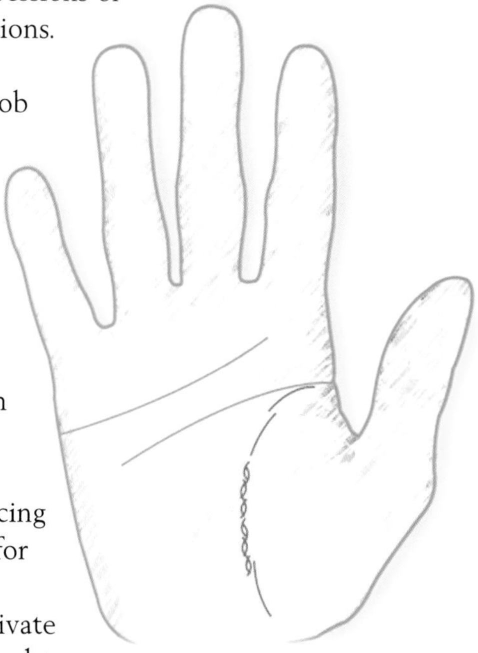

Self-employment may not bring great personal satisfaction. You are easily distracted by new interests, so you must learn to focus your attention. With some inspiration and elbow grease, you can be the best in your field. Grounded feet will help keep your goals in focus.

When it tassels at the wrist. You live on nervous energy. Relax, please! Overly idealistic, you are frequently disappointed because you often see others through rose-colored glasses. Cheerful, upbeat companionship will stimulate your positive feelings. You have a vivid imagination, but don't let it get away from you!

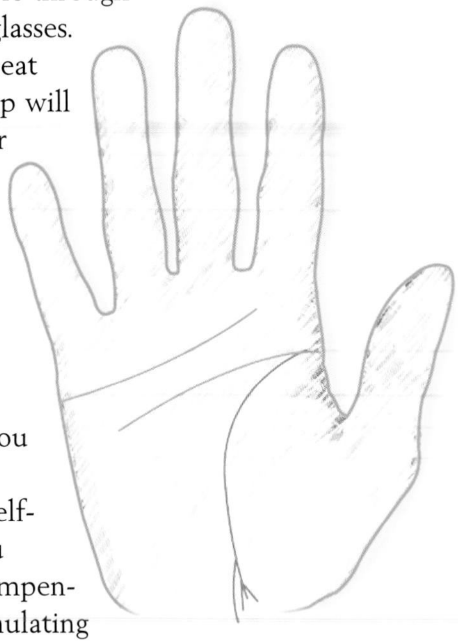

Because you feel insecure about being self-sufficient, you may try to compensate by accumulating material comforts. You usually don't seek the limelight, but you accept it humbly if it comes, knowing you did what anyone would have in the situation. You can succeed as well as others, but you won't unless you are convinced of your abilities.

When your entire Life Line is tasseled or frayed. Take time for yourself. Though generous and giving, you sometimes lose perspective on personal priorities and responsibilities. Highly sensitive, you connect with others on an unconscious, emotional level. You feel what they feel. You must be careful with your friends and support system. Don't worry so much about those around you. Otherwise you'll be easily sucked into others' problems and dilemmas. You're a deep-feeling dreamer, not a bottom-line doer. Refuse to let your imagination run away with you.

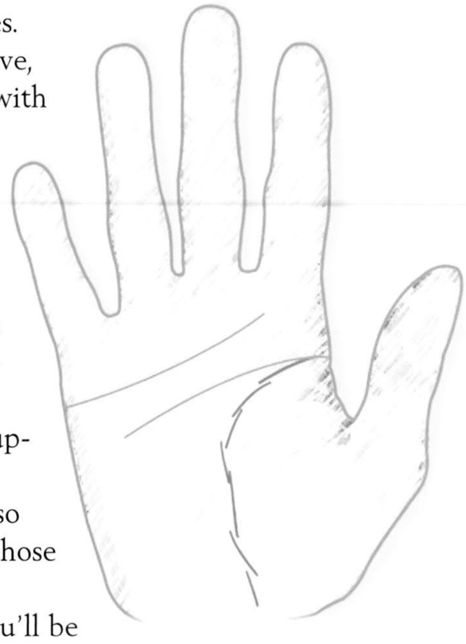

When the line is broad and sweeping and travels into the middle of the palm. You are quick and active and tend to grasp concepts with lightning speed. You're not blinded by rigid attitudes and beliefs; you speak forcefully and loud. Mentally agile and clever, you learn joyously, like a child, always ready for stimulation. But you have difficulty grasping abstract philosophies. Your concern is collecting data, and you're a storehouse of facts and trivia. Try teaching, writing.

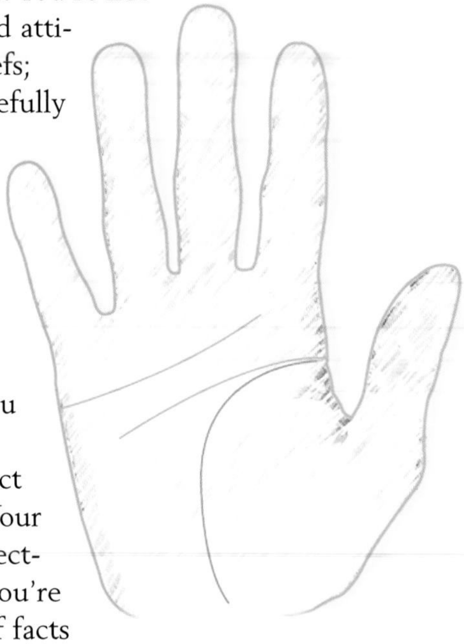

You work independently, not relying on feedback for assurance you're on the right track. Although you have some feelings of insecurity, your need to express your talents in a meaningful endeavor assures your potential success. Don't be afraid to ask questions of people with proven credentials and know-how. You come up short on follow-through; you're often too stubborn to see another point of view.

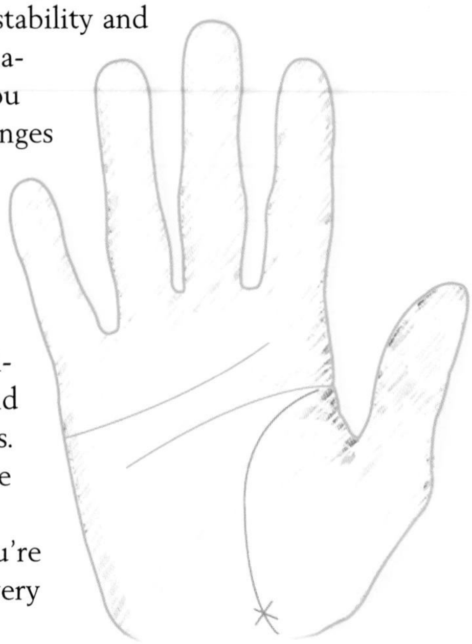

When an X appears at the bottom of the line. You need stability and a sense of permanence in life. You don't make changes quickly or easily. You're a loyal, steadfast partner and friend, but you're also terribly stubborn and set in your ways. Although you're devoted and dependable, you're inclined to be very

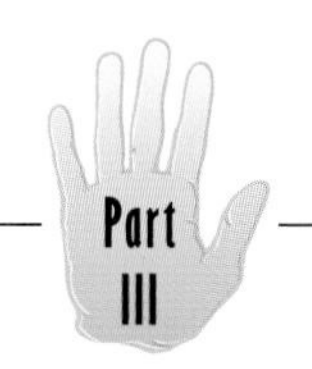

cautious with friends. You tend to do things out of a sense of devotion and duty rather than personal desire and are unwilling to make changes. Don't make impossible demands on yourself or loved ones! Express your true feelings with affection and compassion, and let bygones be just that.

Take advantage of your resourceful mind and develop it into your greatest asset. You are enormously talented in capitalizing on your ideas, but you must avoid people who try to distract you from your goals. Put anxieties on the shelf. Don't allow apathy or indolence to get in your way. The future is yours to shape and mold.

The Head Line

Your quality of mind and intellectual appetite are what the Head Line is all about, not your IQ. Generally speaking, the longer the line, the greater your perceptive abilities and dedication to learning.

When it's deep. The deeper the line, the more you harness your wits and put your know-how to good use. Optimistic and idealistic, you always look for the silver lining and believe things will turn out for the better, if not the best. Talkative and gregarious, you enjoy sharing ideas with others and have the ability to organize and inspire groups of people. Word games, crossword puzzles, and reading are favorite amusements for you. Go easy on yourself. Exert gentle, continual effort toward all goals.

When it's wide and thick. Decision-making is difficult for you. Responsibility isn't your strong suit, and things like car payments and business meetings tend to slip your mind. Passions rule your thinking, often making you act in haste or anger. You have difficulty asserting yourself and going after what you want in a direct, decisive manner. Learning to handle your affairs efficiently will reduce the possibility of losses.

With additional education you can expect your ability to meet challenges to improve greatly. Unless you're as determined to find answers as you are to ask questions, you will be poorly equipped for mental sparring. You're not a quick learner, but what you understand leaves a lasting impression. You will fulfill your creative potentials only when you accept the necessity of painstaking hard work. Returns depend entirely on the investment you can make.

When it resembles a chain-link fence. You're open to new ideas but you insist on the freedom to do things your own way. As a result you sometimes distance yourself from companions and coworkers. A dabbler, you lack organization and perseverance to see projects to completion, rarely acquiring more than a superficial understanding of anything. You believe you're entitled to experience everything life has to offer, and your motto might be "The sky's the limit."

You like being in the company of creative people. Even if you don't have talent yourself, you can spot it in others. Since you love learning and sharing what you know with others, you might excel as a teacher or a lecturer. Being a foreign correspondent might also be your ideal job, allowing you to travel and write about your adventures.

When it ends between the index and middle fingers. You respect knowledge and believe in equality. You're strongly opinionated and never tire of learning new things. Able to focus and productively direct your energies, you don't waste effort, and accomplish more than most people. However, you tend to be a perfectionist, short on patience with everyone's mistakes, including your own.

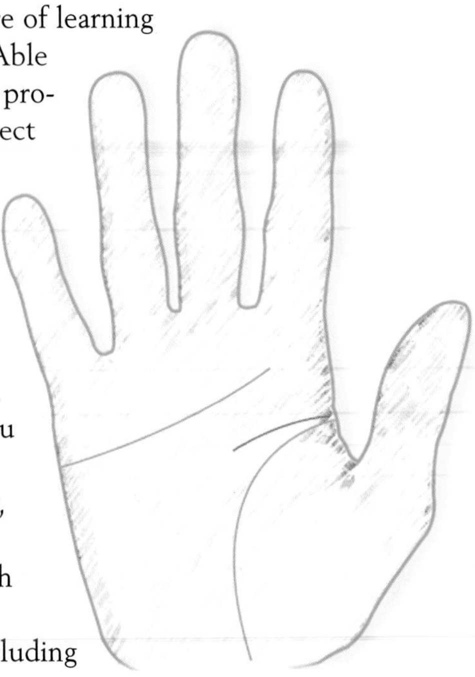

An overly cautious and perfectionist manner can cause you to miss out on spontaneous opportunities. You pursue goals with steady, well-planned steps and attempt only projects that seem to be a sure thing. No flash-in-the-pan schemes for you! Your common sense and practicality should be an advantage in any business area.

When it ends halfway across the palm. You tend to have a one-track mind and can be short-sighted and close-minded. Issues of power and control are likely at play in your life. You assume authority easily and are comfortable with decision-making. You have a penchant for order and self-sufficiency that makes people immediately notice you. Though you might be initially stung by criticism, you never admit defeat and bounce back easily from disappointment.

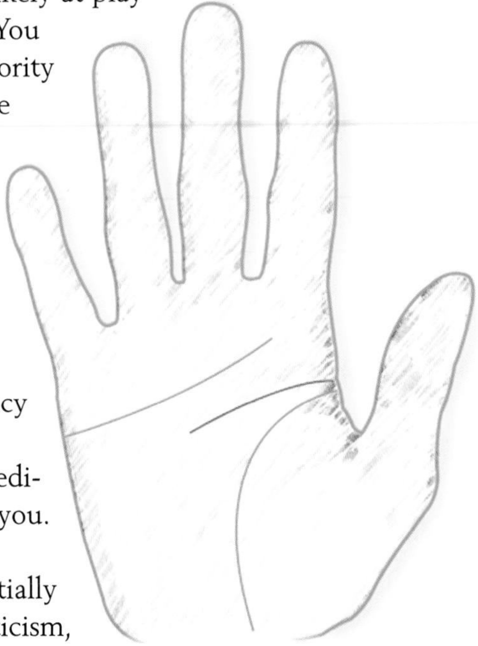

When something needs to be done you are the one who does it, and you manage to accomplish more than most through efficient organization of time and resources. You need to be fully informed at all times so you don't have to take second place to anyone. You might seek security in material wealth and work hard to acquire as many financial assets as possible. This describes the office manager and production supervisor.

When the line is doubled. You have a better ability to combat stress than the average person. Dealing with frustration gives you the determination to withstand future conflicts. Nonetheless, stop grinding your teeth and take a long soak in the hot tub.

Prepare your defenses in depth against emotionally painful rejections, or else your effectiveness will be considerably eroded. You have the ability to make even the most routine job indispensable to reaching your goals. Direct your career efforts to enhancing your money-making efforts. You are confident that everything will work out as planned, because you have laid a good foundation of self-discipline and organization. You will probably find it most comfortable to remain independent in your rise to economic prominence so you can take full advantage of opportunities without having to check with anyone.

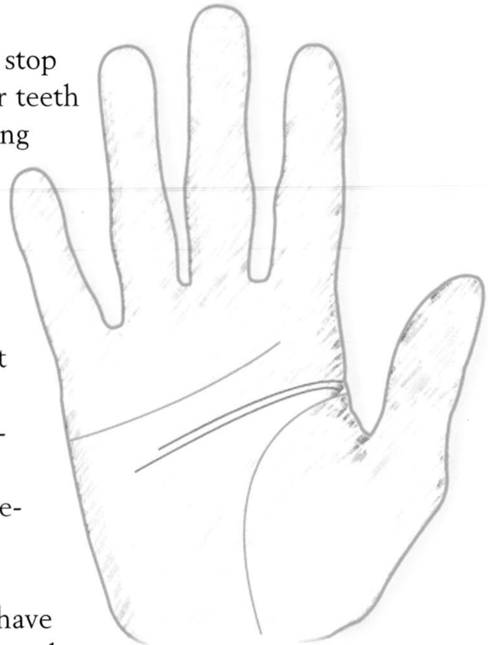

When it starts beneath the Life Line. You're likely to rebel against authority and convention. You aren't afraid of competition because you know it will sharpen your skills. You're very concerned with making the most of your potentials to achieve public status or with those you love. You are a good listener, and others love the way you can serve their needs. The worst thing you could do is lose faith in your ability to reach your goals and objectives. Always on your mind is the fear that you might not live up to other's great expectations. So what?

Friends like being around you because you make them feel welcome and comfortable. You don't make demands, and they can express their opinions freely. You know instinctively what other people need from you, which gives you an edge over your competition. When you have an objective in mind and aren't simply blowing off steam, stay focused. Return favors to helpful friends. Don't alienate those who can help you accomplish what you desire.

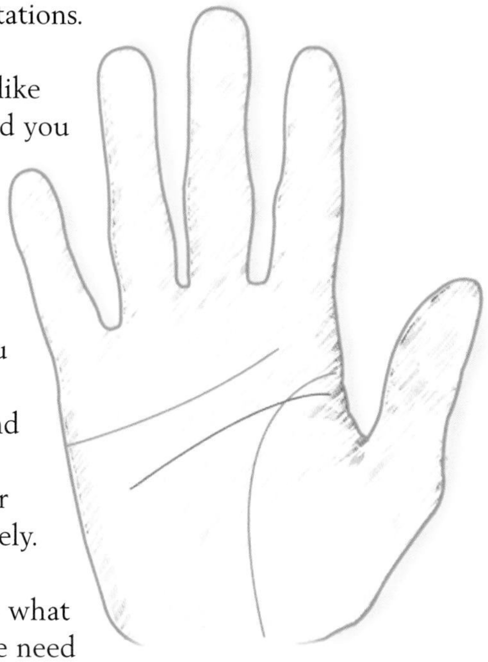

When it begins beneath the index finger. You project an image of self-confidence, self-sufficiency, and vitality that makes people notice you. "What's in it for me?" is your credo. You enjoy being recognized and admired. However, you often fail to realize the needs of others and may turn off those whose adoration and respect you desperately desire.

Highly emotional, you can be rather "touchy," easily upset, and volatile when you don't get your way. You're always ready to stand up and fight for what you believe in. Though you consider yourself open-minded, you really regard your views as the only "right" way. You have the energy and enthusiasm to stir others to action and could be effective as a labor organizer, politician, or community leader.

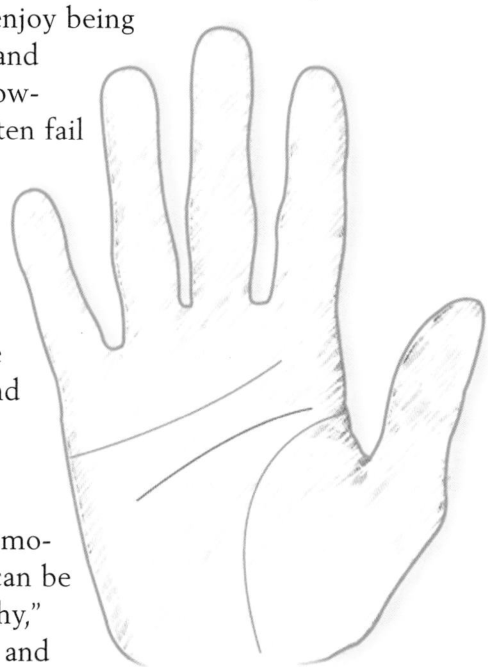

When there is separation between the Head Line and Life Line. This suggests independent thinking but poor follow-through. Although you do everything enthusiastically, you sometimes lack the self-discipline required to get the most from your efforts. Your impatience impedes efficiency, but your aggressiveness works when it's time for action. You're often well informed but unrealistic in your impulsive intellectual outbursts.

You have strong opinions; when your mind is made up, you won't take no for an answer. Think about the goals you hope to reach and remember that achieving them should be the most important priority. Even though you tend to spend money carelessly and get into situations you're not adequately prepared for, avenues for expressing your creative potential are virtually unlimited.

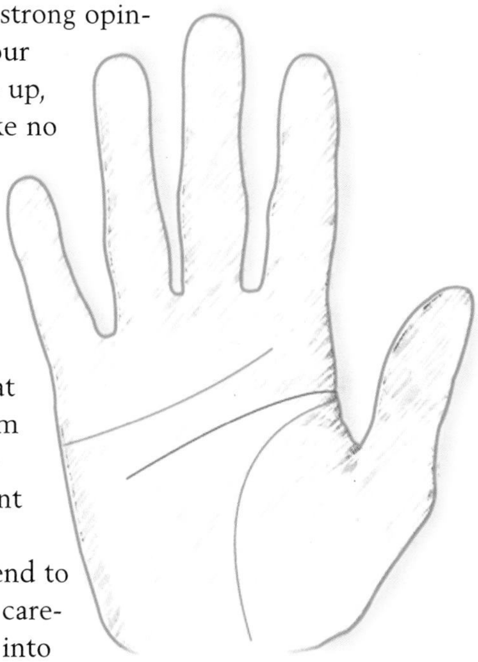

When the Head Line and Life Line are joined at the beginning. You have plenty of common sense, and when it comes down to managerial abilities and planning, nobody does it better! Work is very important to you. Conservative in your views, you resist change and can be rather narrow-minded at times. You expect others to let you do everything your way on your schedule. You're not afraid of responsibility, but you always need assurance that your freedom will not be curtailed if you accept it. You say, "I'll get the job done, my way."

You don't tolerate anyone who violates your trust. You may not be rebellious by nature, but you resent anyone who tries to force you to relinquish control. You know what you want out of life and enjoy the driver's seat. Be more moderate and try to compromise when appropriate. We all need others to help us realize our goals. Make the most of opportunities by demonstrating your creative talents without alienating competitors.

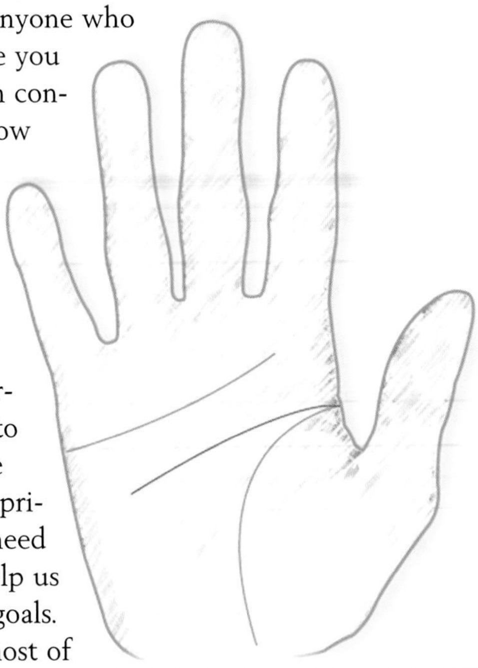

When it travels straight and level across the palm. You're a just-the-facts, cool, and logical type. You hold stubbornly to your beliefs regardless of what others think. Clear thinking is your credo. Serious and at times pessimistic, you can become terribly critical of abstract or revolutionary concepts. Your sights are firmly focused on goals, with few doubts that you will achieve them.

You demand freedom to exploit your ideas so you can prove to yourself and to the world that they are valuable assets. When someone questions your judgment you simply go along by yourself, certain that you will succeed. You are responsive to society's most pressing problems and needs, which suggests a career that involves helping those who are unable to help themselves. Work toward your goals according to a planned program.

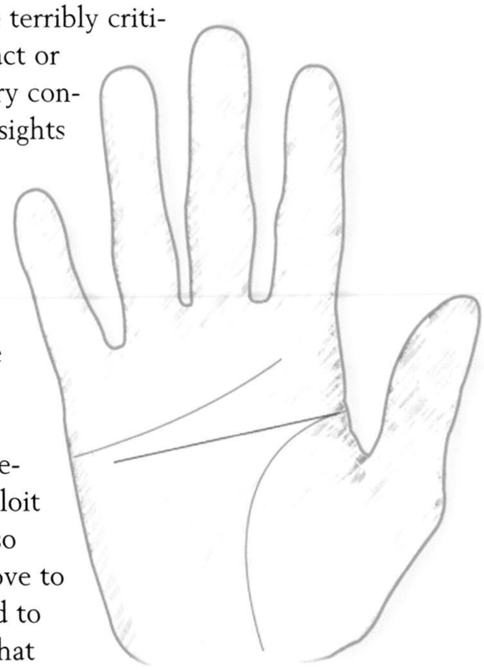

When it's straight and ends in a fork. This reveals an intuitive, quick, inventive nature. The wider the fork, the more resourceful. You are concerned with the world of ideas, particularly the progressive ones. Easily bored, you require high levels of excitement and stimulation. When you believe, you believe passionately and express your ideals with evangelistic zeal. Also known as the "writer's fork," this shows that you're versatile and curious.

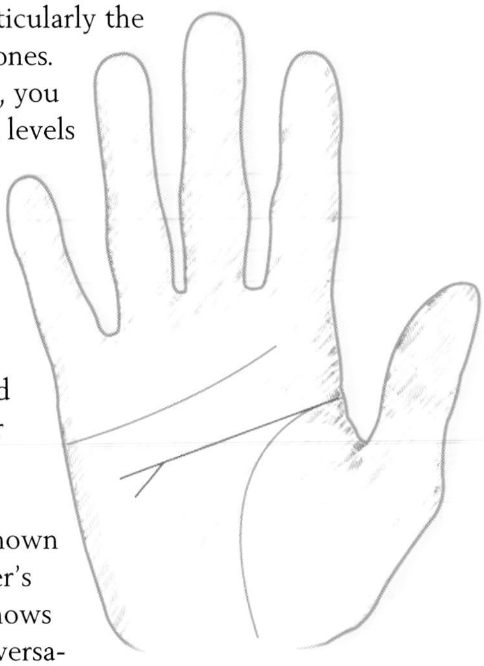

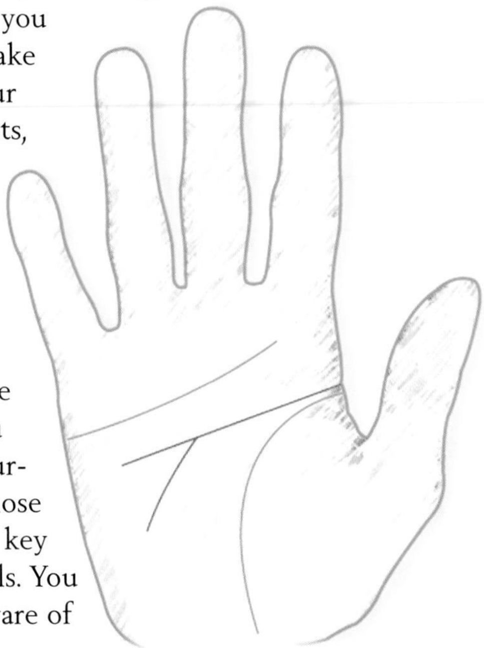

An excessively long fork. This means that you're able to find ways to fulfill the demands of family life while devoting most of your energy to career. It's easy to put your best foot forward with finesse and tact. You enjoy confronting opponents in your struggle to get what you want. You take pride in your achievements, and each success stimulates you to go for more. Because you're a free thinker, you alienate yourself from those who hold a key to your goals. You are fully aware of your impact on those around you, and let everyone know that you are a person of substance. Cool it! Let others talk and throw their ideas around too.

When it takes a sharp upward bend toward the little finger. You use your wits for making money—and lots of it! You rarely say anything you're sorry for later. Time is money, and you get things done while others dream on. Your no-nonsense attitude helps you in all fields and endeavors. You have a driving ambition to make an impression on the world. On the whole, you are concerned with money not as an end but as a means to achieve more rewarding objectives. Plan your actions carefully so you won't be in danger of nervous exhaustion from pushing to meet deadlines.

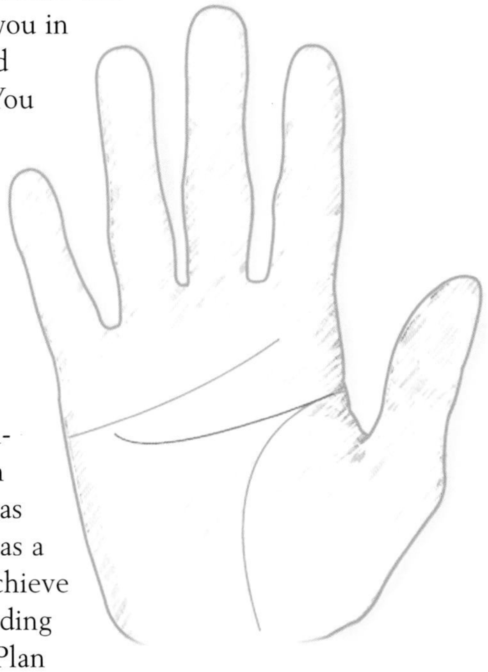

Your ability to detect human weaknesses gives you an advantage over your competition. Learn the art of friendly persuasion. Your bosses may have difficulty getting you to do things their way. But because you can usually justify your position and because you are able to stay with a problem until it's solved, you quickly earn respect. Help people become more self-reliant by teaching them how to take advantage of their own resources and capitalize on natural talents.

When it gently curves downward toward the wrist. You have a good imagination. Lacking attention for mundane matters, you drift in and out of conversations, and your mind seems always preoccupied with something else. Don't let your fantasies ride off with you!

You normally have trouble asserting yourself and tend to be rather withdrawn, even timid (unless your thumb is bulbous and you possess a very large Mount of the Sun under the thumb). Passive and peace-loving, you have no desire to behave aggressively or engage in combat or contest with others. You believe in turning the other cheek. Your temperament is well suited to dealing with people in your daily affairs. You are willing to make concessions to succeed, and your competitors usually cooperate. You don't mind making sacrifices for those you love, but resent being taken for granted as a condition of the relationship. Don't underestimate your abilities or strength in seeing options and alternatives.

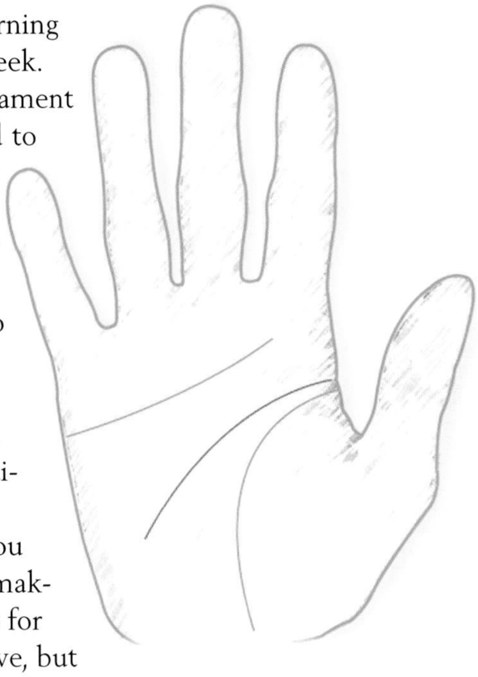

When it plummets to the wrist in a sharp curve. You love fantasy and have an intuitive mind. This is a valuable gift when used artistically or in business. However, your imagination sometimes runs away with you. You're always looking to the future instead of thinking about the here-and-now. You find solace in heartfelt discussions and constantly seek opportunities to share your deepest feelings with others. You might be interested in social work or religious pursuits.

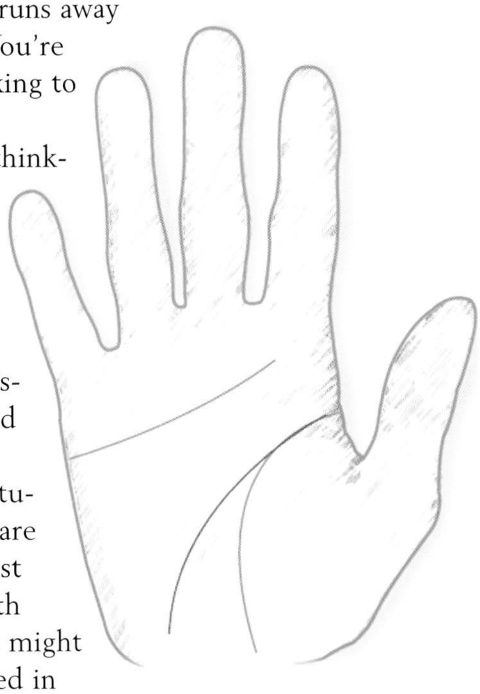

You are extraordinarily sensitive to others, which may frighten you or make you feel vulnerable or defenseless. Don't play the martyr or victim! Your sensitivity enables you to feel a kinship with all living things—people, plants, pets—and you have a keen awareness. Find healthy ways to open up channels between your conscious and subconscious needs.

When it travels straight across the palm to the thumbless side. Because you believe in yourself, you will probably succeed in your endeavors. Not one to let opportunity pass you by, you rise eagerly to every occasion that offers a chance to prove yourself. You will go far if you learn you don't know everything there is to know.

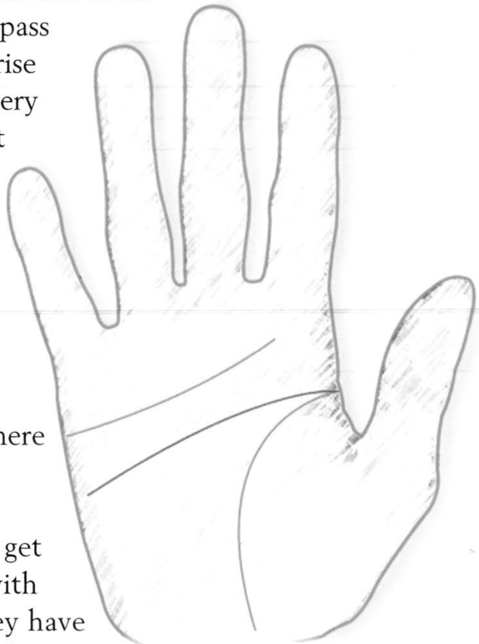

A good listener, you get along well with people if they have something substantial to say. You enjoy small talk but like the bottom line. You will be much happier if you learn to be self-sufficient. It may be difficult separating your priorities from those of loved ones, but workwise you're a pro! A career in counseling people, solo or in groups, would be good. Problem-solving and troubleshooting are your strengths.

When your Head Line and Heart Line join together. Decision-making may not be your strength. People are attracted to you because you make them feel important. You find repetitive jobs useless and boring. You're drawn to occupations in which there is a minimum of routine and you are free to be spontaneous and deal with the public. You want opportunities to grow and be grand. If you don't agree with someone's opinion, you may concede to avoid alienating him.

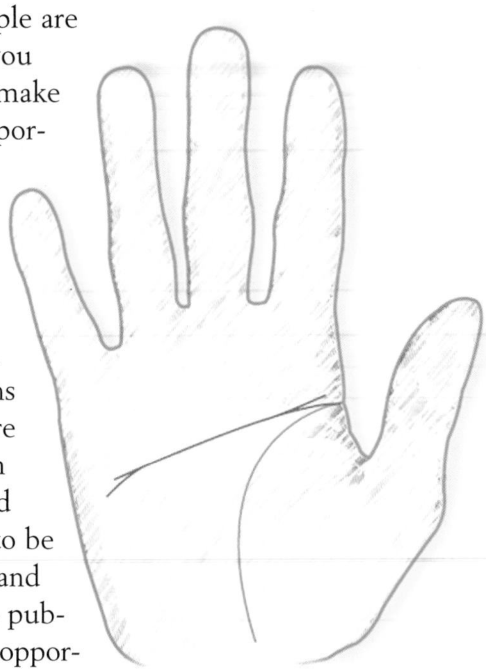

You were impatient growing up because you couldn't wait to display your creative potential. You'll help improve the quality of life for many people by sharing your people skills with those who want to better their station in life. Allow others to make decisions and learn by adversity. Don't let corporate decisions drive you crazy. You know what you want. Just be patient and accommodating.

When the line descends near the end. You may have difficulty seeing loved ones as individuals, separate from yourself. They're your babies, your possessions, your treasures. *Yours*, you say. Lighten up! You're preoccupied with having what you want and on your terms. You enjoy life's comforts but may think of family as nothing more than devoted pets. Don't let your preoccupation with security and schedule-keeping interfere with your private life. Avoid making comparisons with other people and expecting everyone to dance to your tune. Let others be themselves.

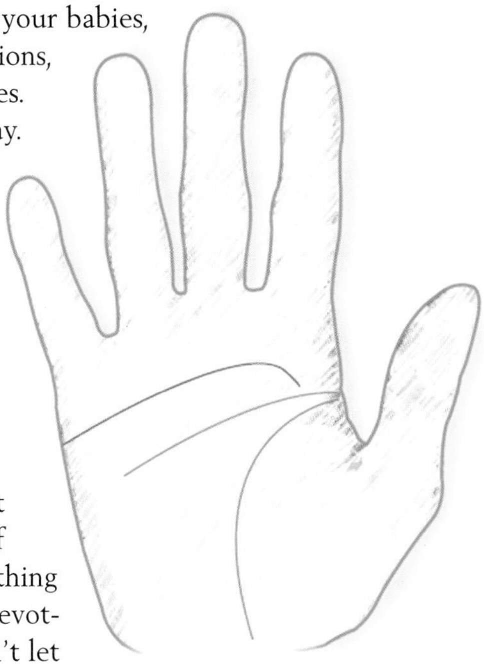

Your goals are always well defined. You waste little time getting your career plans under way to achieve your aims as soon as possible. You're not the easy-come, easy-go type. Accept the daily trials of the real world and try seeing people as people, not possessions. Remember, "being" is as important as "having." Reserve time for love. Explore it.

When it suddenly appears between the little and index fingers. You have great skills at courting and love-making. You have the ability to see both sides of a drama and usually find an optimistic, happy ending to every story. You're more fair and equitable than most, and may make a good judge, mediator, lawyer or even umpire.

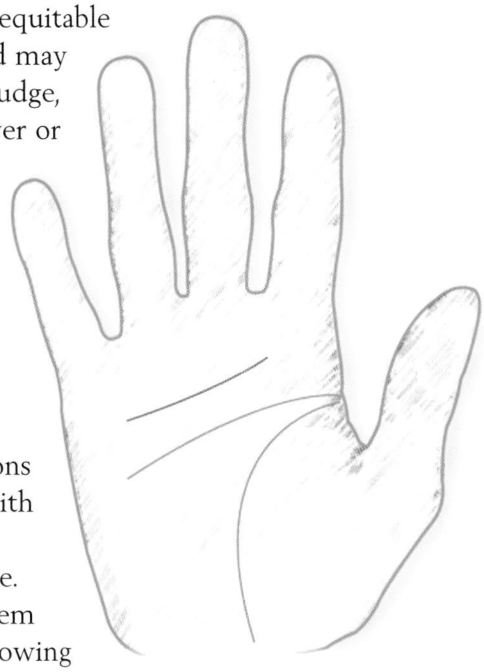

Because you can see the plus and minus of everything, however, you have trouble making decisions and sticking with the ones you finally do make. One big problem you have is allowing others to make up your mind for you, because you tend to idealize romantic attachments. You want love and attention and affection and you may sacrifice your needs for theirs. Develop some firm convictions of your own. What do *you* want?

When this short line hugs the base of the fingers. You don't like causing friction or being disagreeable. At best, you're willing to serve and give; at worst, you're vacillating and weak-willed.

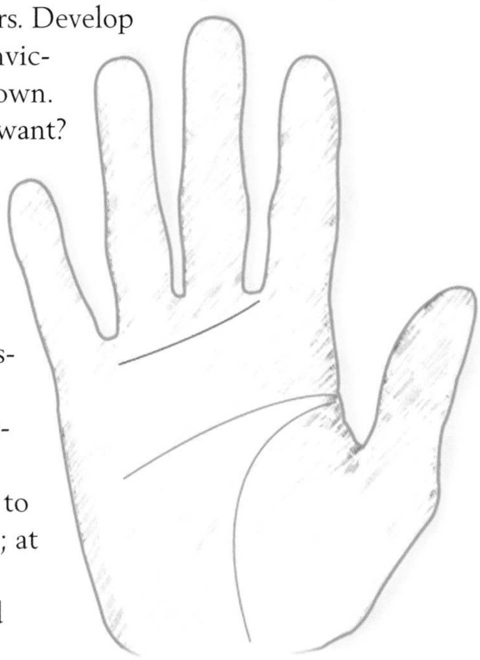

Minor Lines

Every palm differs in the number and nature of its lines. Some hands don't have any minor lines. For those that do, here are the most common ones.

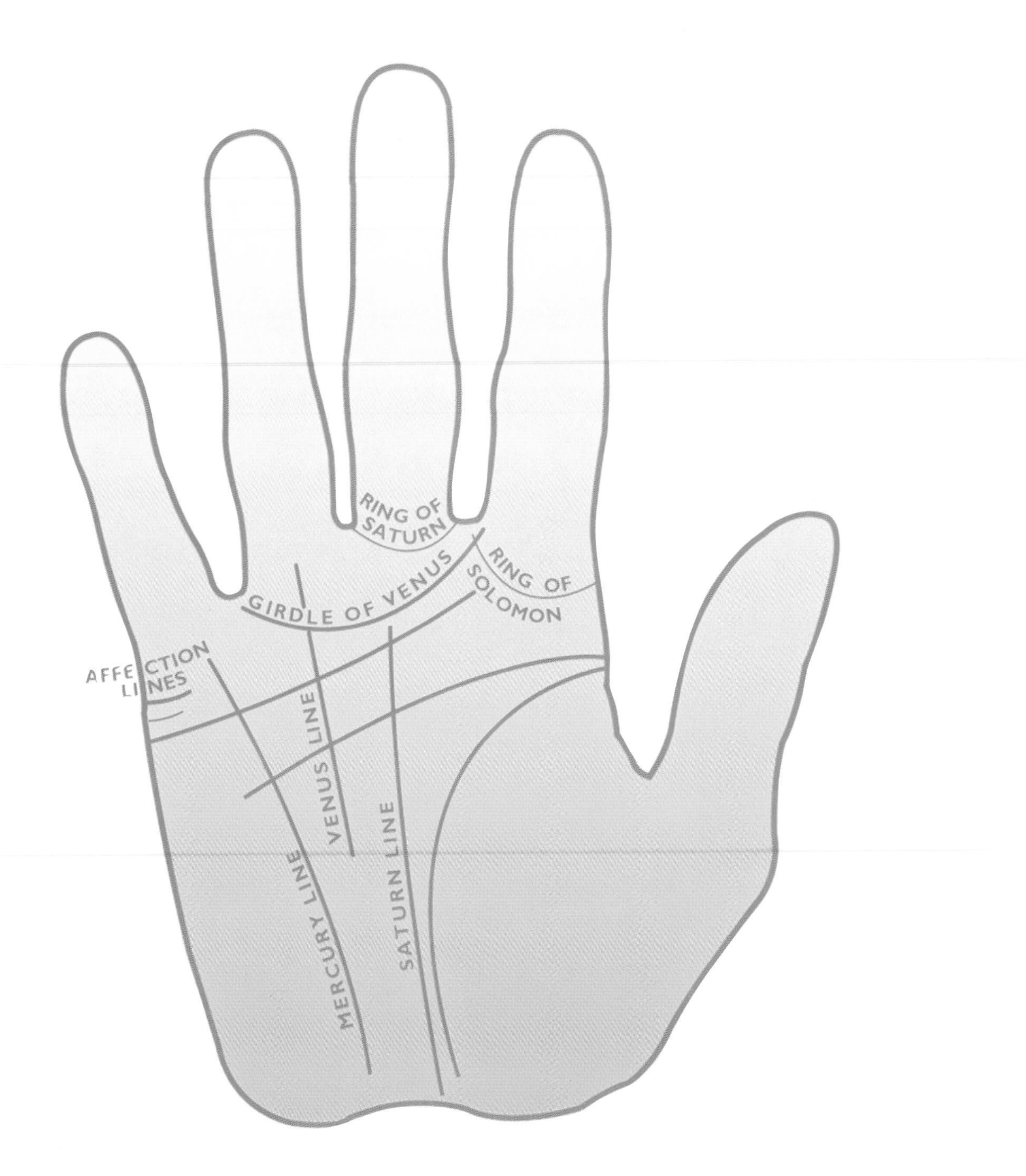

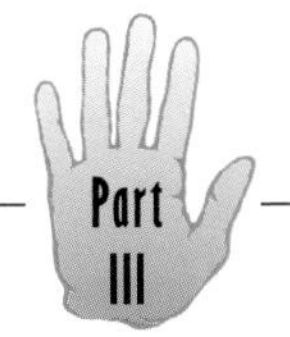

The Saturn Line

Also known as the Fate Line, the Saturn Line is found in only 40 percent of all palms. It is composed of two or more vertical lines running upward from the wrist to the middle finger, frequently veering off course between the Head and Heart Lines. Saturn Lines say how you feel about the material world, your economic opportunities, and your ability to follow a course of action. It has nothing to do with predestination.

If you have no Saturn Line. Don't fret! It's likely you associate with people like yourself and from whom you know what to expect. You can always be depended on to aid a friend in need. You like the tried-and-true and rarely take chances. You like things to go as planned, on schedule. You're *not* an eccentric.

When it's long, clear, and straight, ending at the base of the middle finger. You have a sense of contentment with the material world, and daily structure prevails. The urge to acquire dignity and perks and to be self-sufficient in work commands much of your attention. Normally your emotional poise makes you win over adversaries. Take advantage of your natural talents to gain the security you need to feel comfortable with your accomplishments and needs. The worst thing you can do is yield to family pressure or work ties and deny yourself the opportunity to prove that you are capable of succeeding without interference from them. Your progress depends largely on establishing your independence and self-determination.

When it's broken, split, or faded. These patterns denote a desire for money and recognition. You put a great deal of energy into acquiring life's necessities. You strive for security and independence, and avoid relying on others.

When it's composed entirely of broken fragments. This suggests a poor business sense. Research! You need things well organized and clearly defined but may be incapable of doing it on your own.

When it curves away from the thumb and toward the little finger. You have a strong need to be needed. Be more aggressive in promoting yourself and your ideas, and don't be afraid to let others know you can't be used. Live up to your potential and capitalize on your resources to achieve financial security. Avoid comparing your own achievements with those of others. Be happy with what you've been able to do. Use some self-esteem and elbow grease!

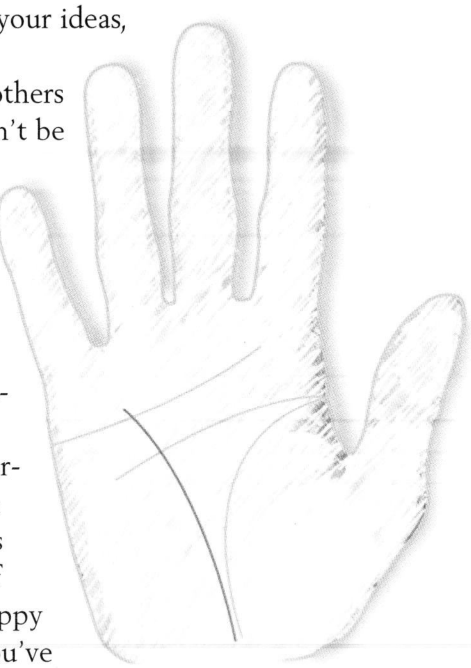

When it's made up of two or more lines, clear or broken. You work best in partnerships, both romantic and business. You're good at organizing others. Cautious by nature, you take time to plan your moves carefully, but you adjust quickly and learn new skills and methods when necessary. Basically honest and sincere, you win the respect and confidence of friends and colleagues easily. Many of your tests and financial hurdles involve home and family.

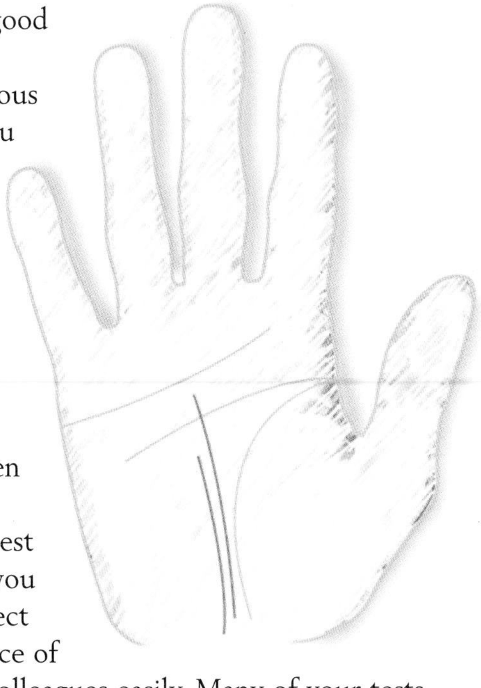

When the line (or one of its forks) starts within the Life Line. Your physical home is your source of stability and security. A traditionalist, you cling tightly to conservative opinions. You prefer to do things by the book. Gaining financial and emotional security is a high priority. When you have this marking, you're likely to benefit from inheritance or financial assistance from relatives. Allow room to grow, because once you get started, you're never content until you fulfill your maximum potential.

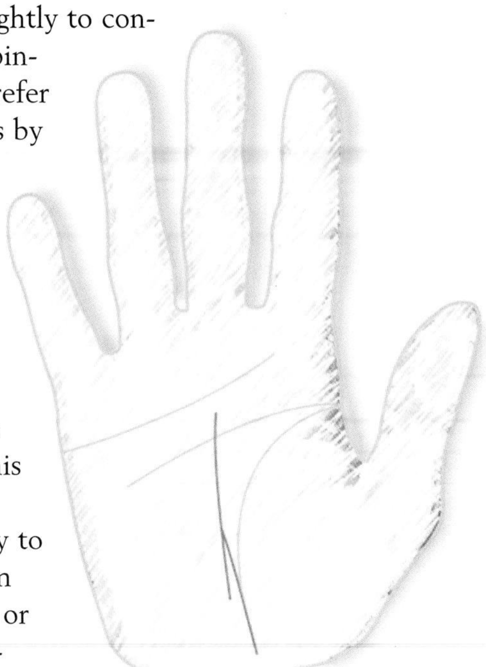

When it ends at the Head Line. You have trouble separating your emotions from rational thought. Although you have strong ties to your family and a deep sense of responsibility to them, you recognize the importance of standing on your own. Your sense of humor may help you survive experiences that might otherwise leave you emotionally crushed.

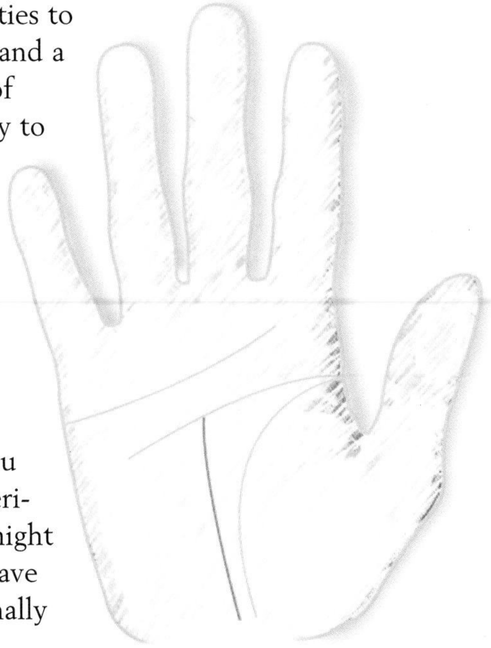

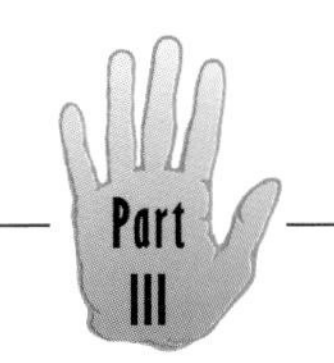

When it ends at the Heart Line. You have more faith in yourself than in anyone else. Life's hassles are likely to stem from a poor choice of partners or lovers. Your thoughts often center on what people think. You have a deep need to relate to others, professionally and socially, and you derive great satisfaction from indulging those around you. Knowing you've been helpful makes you feel good, but you need to remember to look out for Number One.

When it veers toward the index finger. Public success or recognition from peers is in your future. Dreams, ideals, concepts, and philosophies mean a lot. Because you're adventurous and believe you can succeed, you probably will. You have a talent for getting people to open up to you and reveal information you may someday find useful. Personal satisfaction depends on approval and public opinion.

When there are crosses or chains on the line. This reveals difficult times and periods of uncertainty. Early struggles are located nearest the wrist; obstacles late in life are closer to the base of the middle finger. These markings tell of ambivalent feelings and a need for cooperation and help.

When the line is wavy. This can indicate a disorganized, quarrelsome personality. Never content, you believe everyone else's garden is greener. You play to win but often ignore integrity and personal well-being, so keep an eye on stress factors! You don't like radical concepts and prefer firm foundations, with an eye for endurance. Though your friendships may be few, they are usually long-standing.

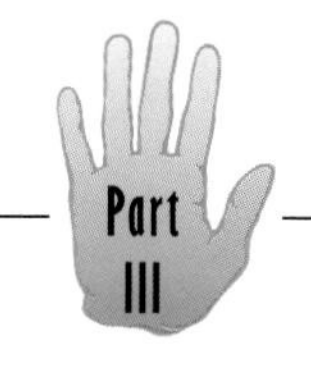

The Venus Line

Lines traveling upward from the middle of the palm to the ring finger are called Venus Lines. Here is where you gain insight into how you apply yourself on the job and what your best vocational abilities might be.

When it's long and straight. This suggests career brilliance. You can be quite charming and something of a flatterer when it suits your purposes. Social, outgoing, and extremely communicative, you talk to anyone who'll listen and see every conversation as an opportunity to grow and prosper.

When it starts low on the thumbless side of the palm (the Mount of Moon) and ends below the ring finger. You will most likely receive help from your family. You're attentive, affectionate, and loyal to those you love. Your early conditioning was important in your rise to prominence. Be careful not to fall into ruts and routine. Whatever career you choose, be certain you have enough room to grow and develop to your fullest.

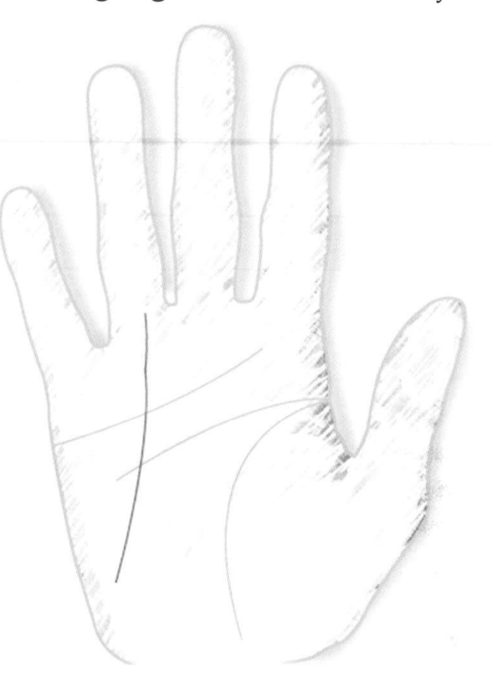

When there are several Venus Lines. This suggests that, although you may have your fingers in many financial pies, you'll eventually succeed on your own merits and individuality. Your assimilate information easily and are knowledgeable about a wide variety of subjects. You make the most of circumstances to further your ambitions by using your well-developed creative imagination and versatility.

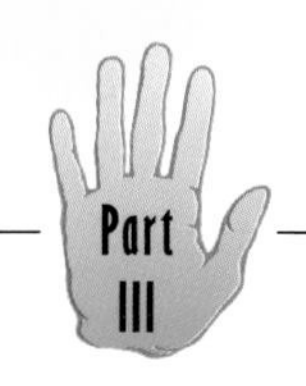

coarse behavior, you tend to turn the other cheek (or get tremendously cool and sarcastic) when situations turn gray. For you, a broken heart or an emotional drama can be fatal.

When deep and well etched and made up of only one or two broken lines, you have a keen imagination and sensitivity to color, sound, and taste. Several small lines traveling toward the little finger warns of hypersensitivity in love relationships; your capacity to delude yourself is strong.

Ring of Saturn

A line or series of lines encircling the middle finger above the Heart Line is call the Ring of Saturn. Its owner is usually philosophically conservative, holding on to traditional ideas and beliefs, and is not easily swayed or influenced by popular opinion or the attitudes of others.

Ring of Solomon

A horizontal line or series of lines below the index finger is called the Ring of Solomon. Its presence says your mind is always active, always seeking. Often found on the hands of teachers and writers.

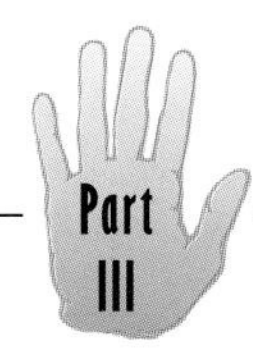

The Mounts

Common Markings

All palms carry a variety of markings. The more pronounced and definite their design, the deeper their impact on your personality. The elevated areas below every finger are called mounts. Their markings either exaggerate or diminish traits attributed to the finger above them (for example, the index, self-esteem; middle finger, structure and schedule; and so forth). Consider your major palm lines as major throughways and markings on the mounts as places of interest.

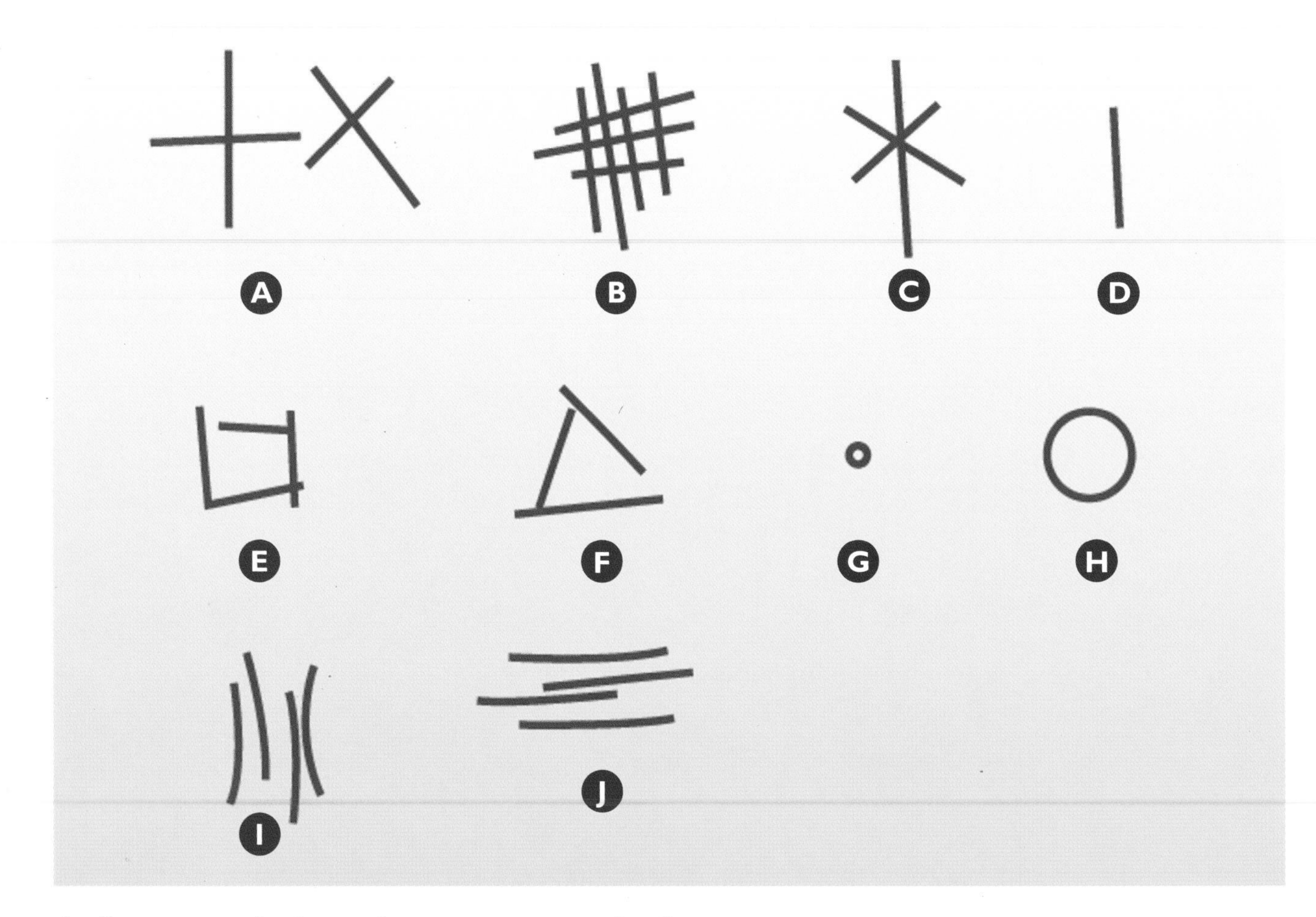

A. Crosses emphasize and exaggerate opposing forces.
B. Grids, like a tic-tac-toe game, either diminish or embellish, depending on where they fall.
C. Five- or six-pointed configurations, called stars, yearn for appreciation and symbolize success.
D. A vertical line, or bar, suggests obstruction.
E. Square formations suggest self-interest and protection.
F. Triangles bring good fortune and a calming influence.
G. Dots dininish energy and can symbolize insomnia and depression.
H. Circles suggest confinement or restriction.
I. A series of vertical lines suggests strength.
J. Horizontal lines resembling minus signs diminish certain qualities or hold them in control.

The Mount of Jupiter

An elevated Mount of Jupiter suggests a love of new ideas and concepts, and good self-esteem.

A cross. This warns against scattering your energies; desired goals may not get recognized due to too many fingers in too many pies.

A series of horizontal lines. This speaks of big dreams but little initiative.

A star. Indicates happiness with family and support from friends.

A square or one deep horizontal line. This speaks of your ability to intellectually stimulate those around you. Good for teachers and salespeople.

Several vertical lines or a triangle. This accentuates ambition and the need to succeed.

A grid. This warns of egotism, pushiness.

A dot. This indicates a need to be popular.

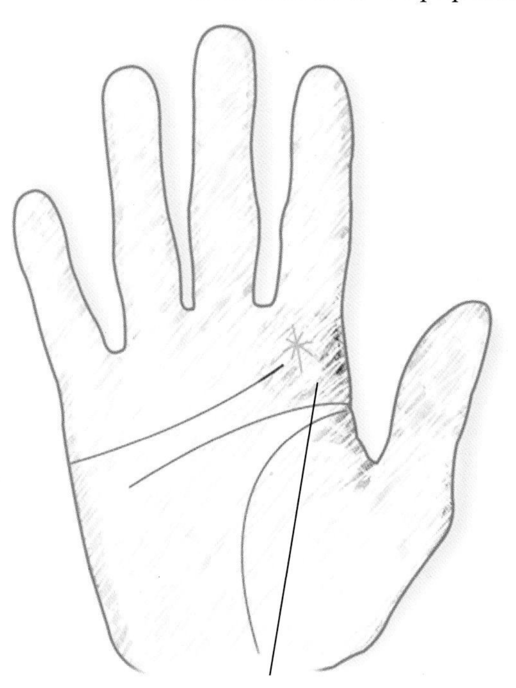

Mount of Jupiter

The Mount of Saturn

An elevated Mount of Saturn indicates a love of structure but warns against melancholia.

A cross. This says watch your step and your mouth and what you put in it! This is the sign of the hypochondriac and the accident-prone.

A series of horizontal lines. This suggests pessimism.

A star. This reflects emotional drama, but also the ability to rise above difficulties. Quite loquacious, you aren't the greatest listener. You're an impractical dreamer—always thinking, not always doing.

Several vertical lines or a triangle. This says you're a curious type open to alternatives and changing ways.

A square. This says you enjoy your quiet time; you're independent and not overly reliant on others.

One deep horizontal line. This shouts independence. Try not to get hung up on schedule and what's supposed to happen; be more spontaneous!

A grid. This tells of comfort with tried-and-true methods. You like being right and don't shun responsibility. This marking can also indicate the need for financial security and personal freedom.

A dot. This mark signifies rebelliousness.

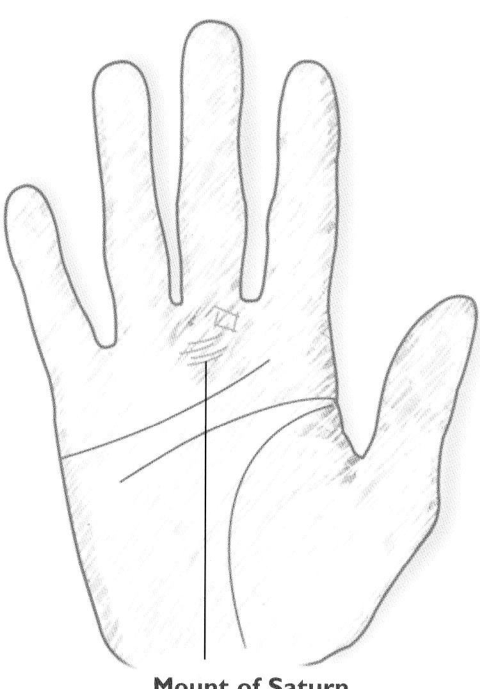

Mount of Saturn

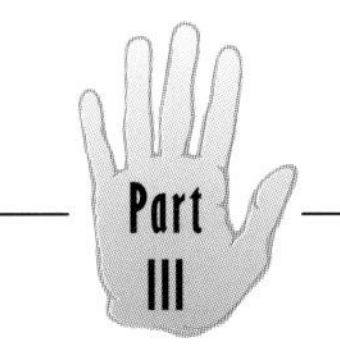

The Mount of Venus

An elevated Venus mount reveals versatility in career and the ability to work well with others.

A cross. This says you're hard-working and yearn for success. People respect you for who you are and what you know. However, success comes in your later years.

A series of horizontal lines. Be discreet with your support system. You stretch yourself thin socially and creatively, and need more discipline.

A star. This is the traditional mark of success attributable to help from others in high places.

A square or one deep horizontal line. This warns you may try too hard and must learn to say no. Surround yourself with positive, successful types only.

Several vertical lines or a triangle. This suggests a restless spirit and happiness from several lines of work. You bore easily, and always have your ear (as well as your nose) to the grindstone looking for better economic and artistic avenues of expression.

A grid. This indicates that your self-discipline is low.

A dot. This suggests your dissatisfaction with your career.

The Mount of Mercury

An elevated Mount of Mercury reveals good business sense and a desire to know facts.

A cross. This reveals hyperactive energy and a potentially sensitive digestive system.

A series of horizontal lines. This says you go in circles, rarely completing what you begin. You have many humanitarian interests but only skim the surface.

A star. This indicates distinction in science and a natural aptitude for business.

A square or a deep horizontal line. This says you are charismatic, opinionated, self-assured, and open-minded.

Several vertical lines or a triangle. This suggests an attraction to writing or the healing arts. Your bedside manner is wonderful! Stand by your opinions and beliefs, and don't let anyone sway you.

A grid. You're greedy for approval—don't martyr yourself. You also have a tendency to misconstrue what others say and are a poor judge of character.

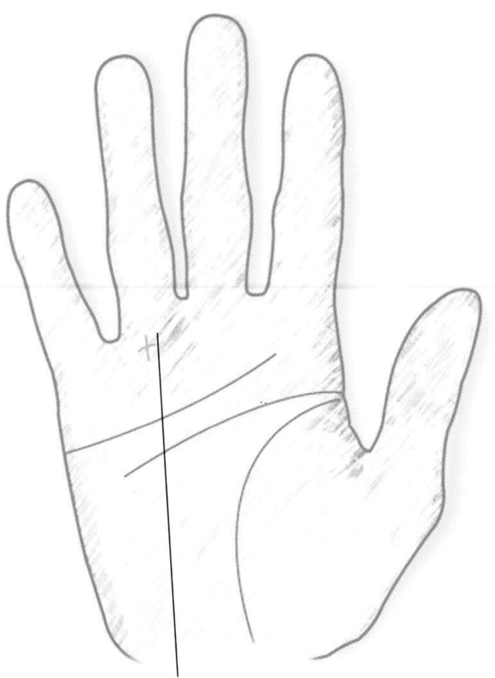

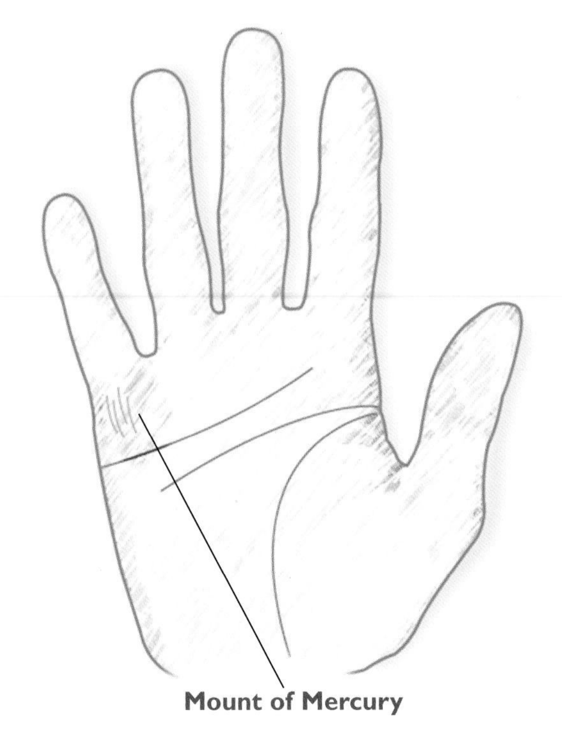

The Mount of Sun

An elevated Mount of the Sun suggests good physical strength and vitality. One that's sunken or low suggests shyness and introversion.

A cross. This speaks of strong self-control and open-mindedness. You possess an indomitable spirit and irrepressible confidence in survival. *Your* way! Take time to plan and don't dwell on past mistakes.

A series of horizontal lines. You like sharing responsibilities and work best with others and in relationships. Not a loner, you are capable of inspiring (or pushing) others to succeed.

A star. This says you are energetic and can accomplish more than most rivals. However, you are self-absorbed and usually don't place much value on other's abilities. You work best solo.

A square or triangle. You view yourself as the center of your own personal universe. You're always ready with an opinion (or a joke) and don't shirk responsibility. Good for teachers and salespeople.

Several vertical lines. These are common on the thumb's lower elevated section. Whether you respect their intelligence and individuality or not, you enjoy sharing with others. However, instead of intellectualizing about philosophy, you respond according to how things "feel." If it feels right, it's a go.

A grid. Highly impressionable, you sometimes use bad judgment in business because you evaluate situations too personally and can't be objective.

A dot. This denotes insomnia—especially if it's red.

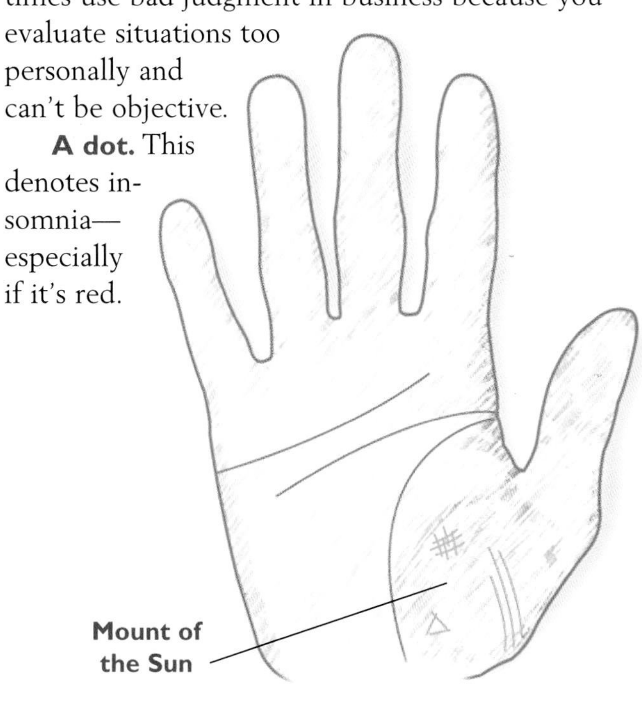

The Mount of the Moon

An elevated Mount of the Moon increases sensitivity and imagination.

A cross. This suggests that you are extremely sensitive and easily hurt. Hindu palm readers say this mark suggests fear of large bodies of water, probably from past lives that ended in drowning or violence. You are easily overwhelmed by emotions and may erect all sorts of defensive barriers to protect yourself from fear and pain.

A series of horizontal lines. This reveals intuitive, supersensitive insights into others. Your gut responses are usually on target.

A star. This indicates your heart rules your head; domination by emotions makes for troubled, irrational decisions. You're full of emotional intensity.

A square. This says you're the one who gets things done. You have good recall and rarely take chances with money, time, emotions or resources.

Several vertical lines, a grid, or a triangle. This says you don't make friends easily. Though your friendships may be few, they are usually long-standing and firm. You like good meals, good surroundings, and deep and good conversation. Perhaps you neglect your material responsibilities, focusing instead on artistic, emotional, philosophical, or individualistic pursuits. Material concerns are attractive but not your priority.

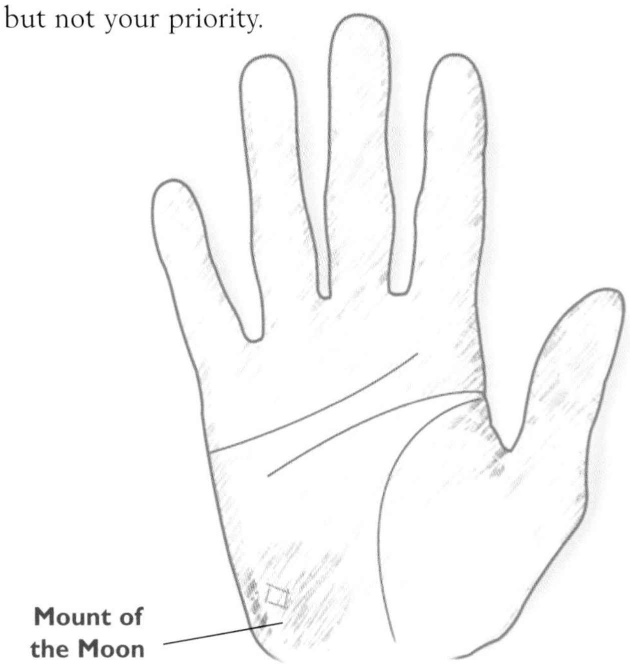

Part IV
Sample Readings

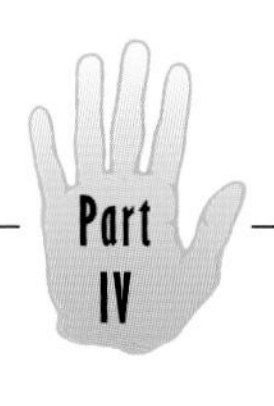
Part
IV

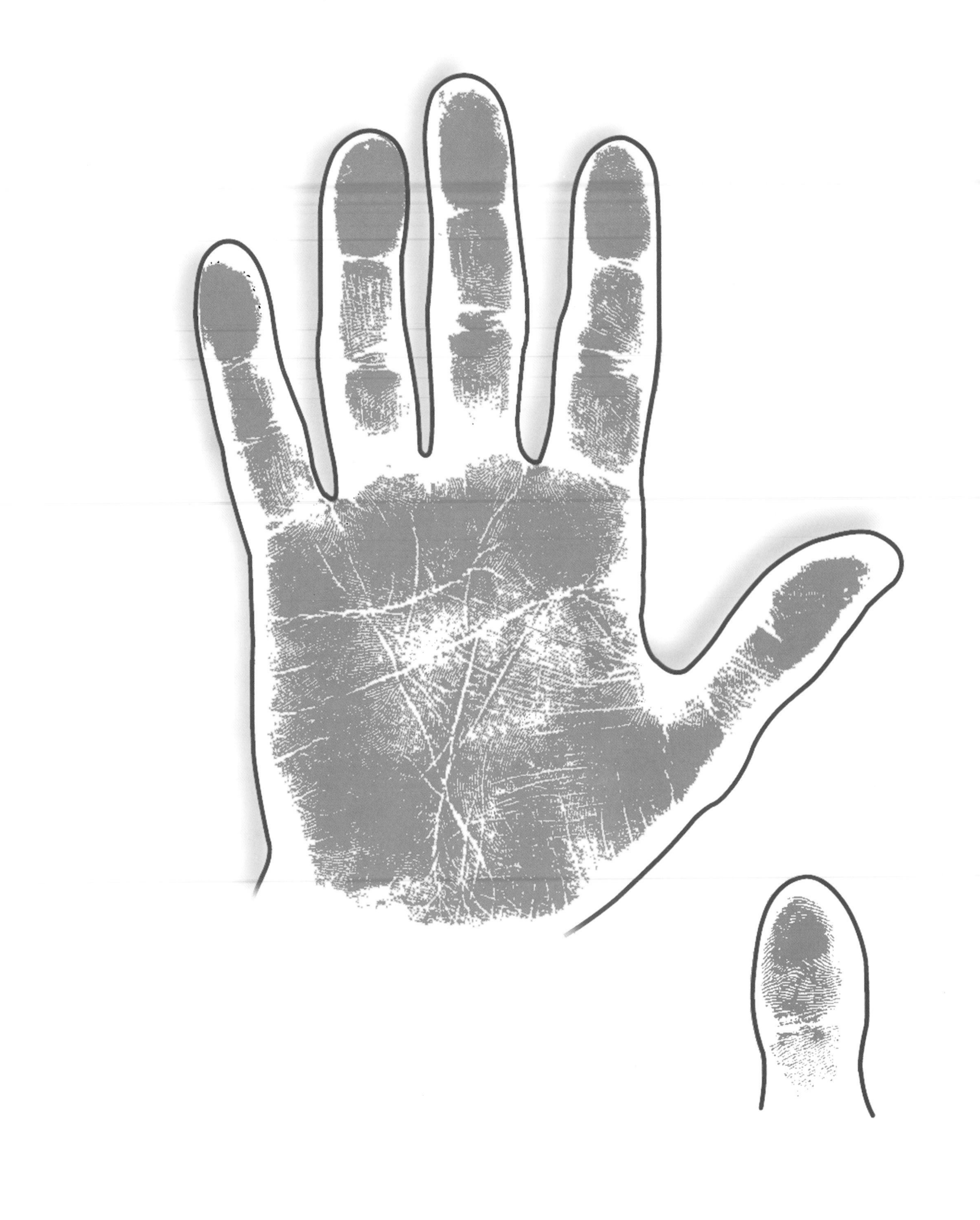

The Right Hand of Mary Brooks

Age 63; a residential and commercial cleaning entrepreneur. Both hands feature rounded, flexible fingers; elastic skin; whorls on all fingers; and pink, almond-shaped nails with no white spots.

The length and roundness of the overall hand and fingertips say your mental stimulation comes from within; your mind is focused on personal or internal issues rather than what the outside world believes. You know what others are thinking but never forget who you are or where you're heading. The upper portion of the ring finger leaning toward the middle one says you look at work relationships as investments and expect a good return; you don't waste time—or money.

A small index finger indicates you are not the type to monopolize conversations and you don't relish the leading role, even though you're not afraid of responsibility (with the support from the dominant lower Saturn and upper Venus Lines). Your strong Mercury Line reveals a knack for saying the right thing at the right time. You truly enjoy helping others by making their life easier and serving their basic needs.

Whorls on all fingers keep you a freethinker, unafraid to champion unpopular causes. You view both love and work as contests and strive diligently for what you believe. No markings on Jupiter's mount beneath the index finger says that with those you care about you are generous to a fault. The highly placed Affection Line beneath the little finger hints of a cautious, practical approach to love. Solid, down-to-earth relationships that provide you with basic needs are better than storybook romances or fly-by-night affairs.

The long Head Line reveals that your mind is always active and, that you pursue every idea that comes along; it's straightness says you don't waste words or engage in frivolous small talk. Even though your dominant fingerprint type is the freethinking whorls, the level and straight angle of the Head Line prevails, keeping you in touch with conservative philosophies. The absence of several small minor lines indicates you like things to be clearly defined; you're a doer, the one who brings the dreamer's vision into being.

A Life Line joined to the Head Line says your mind works in an orderly, organized fashion, carefully calibrating your thoughts, and that you're a stickler for schedule. Because the Life Line splits midway and travels toward the middle of the palm, you're likely to feel wanderlust and want to live in areas away from your origin of birth.

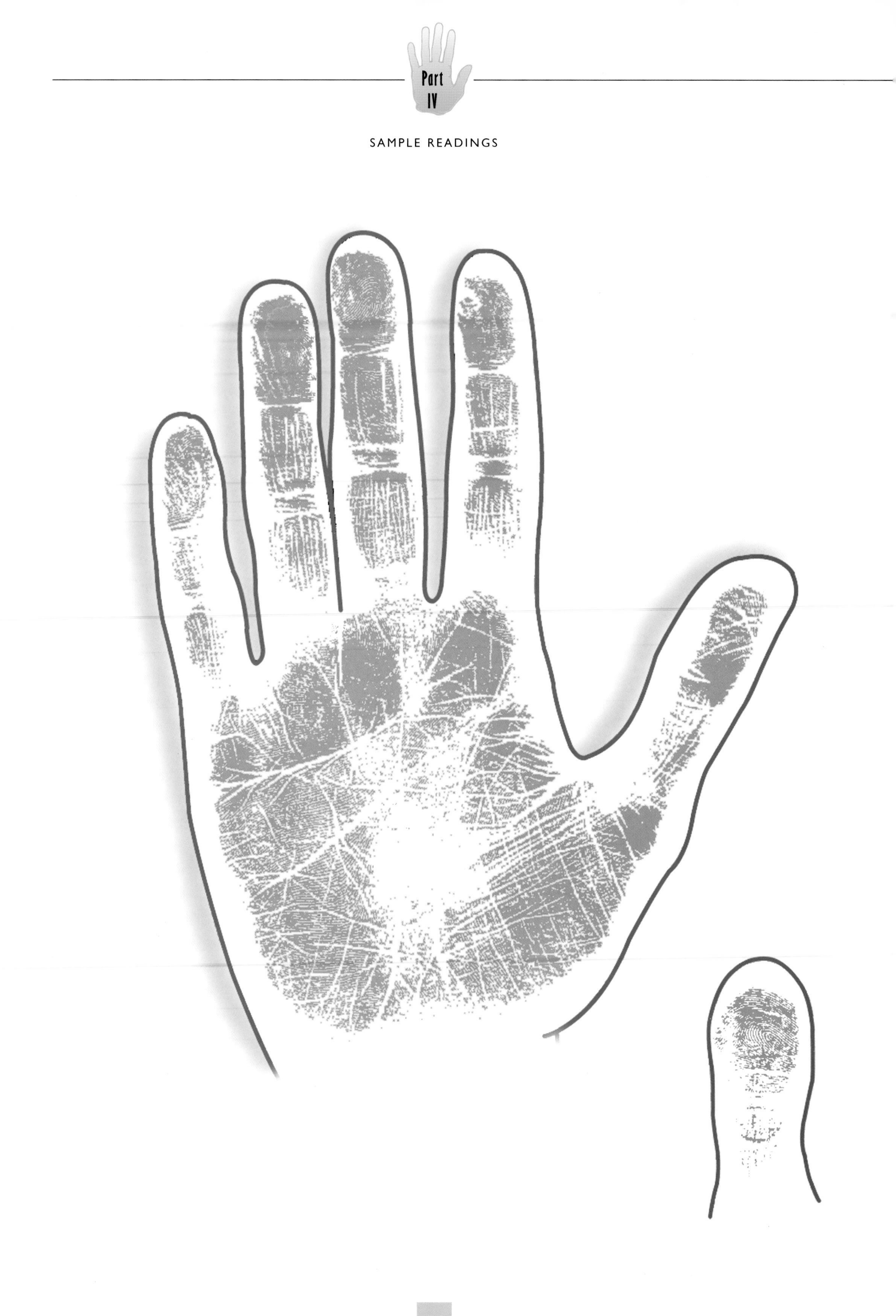

The Right Hand of Sam Green

Age 57; a computer designer/engineer. Both hands feature many lines, rounded fingertips, and arched fingerprints. The skin is elastic but the fingers are rather inflexible, with large square nails filled with white spots.

What a mess of lines! (Remember: the more little lines a person has, the more emotional pies he has his fingers in.) Learn to relax and prioritize, Sam. You're infinitely curious and want to know something about everyone and everything. Your mind never stops buzzing; try meditation, saunas, and exercise.

Long straight fingers say you have a penchant for detail and are precise. However, the long index (Jupiter) digit hints that sometimes you carry your meticulousness to extremes, overworking everything. Arched fingerprints warn against missing the big picture because you're inclined to overdo.

The several forks and branches from your Heart Line says your motto is "The sky's the limit." Your thirst to experience relationships keeps you hungry for more. Because you're good- natured and friendly, it's likely your social contacts are wide and your appointment book is full. You enjoy being in the company of others who are as busy as you.

The straight yet downward angle of your Head Line says that unless something has stood the test of time, you don't place much value on it. Old-fashioned, proven techniques bring you happiness and security. Beware that your overly long index (Jupiter) finger could stimulate your ambitions to do just about anything to achieve your goals, believing that your ends justify the means. You're not a quitter!

The large and supple thumb reveals that growth and expansion are linked to your self-expression. The Ring of Solomon below and circling the index finger mount forewarns that you have a strong sense of the dramatic and can be quite determined in the way you go about expressing yourself. You're not shy; optimism contributes to your successes.

The straight upward Saturn Line combined with the myriad of several tiny lines warn that one of the things you fear most is loss of liberty. You are very defensive about your rights to do what you feel; you clamp down on yourself and everyone else.

Conclusion

Our hands—their lines and peculiarities—tell tales for anyone who has learned to read them. Now you've got the keys to reveal some of life's secrets—right in the palm of your hand. Use your new skills to enrich your life and to better understand yourself and others.

Open hands bespeak open minds.

Glossary

Apollo, Mount of The fleshy area beneath the thumb that reveals your physical stamina and sensual nature. The higher and more firm the area, the greater your capacity to enjoy life and its pleasures.

Affection Lines Also called Marriage Lines. Located below the little finger, these horizontal lines are sometimes intersected by vertical lines and suggest whether love is in your near or far future and what quality your love affairs possess.

Angle of the thumb The wider the distance between the thumb and the side of the palm, the more open-minded and individualistic you are. The smaller its gap, the more conventional.

Bars A series of vertical lines found on mounts that suggests strength.

Bracelets Also called rascelettes, these are horizontal markings above the wrist on the palm side of a hand. When the top one peaks upwards like a pyramid, it's said to reveal vanity, a love of self. In most hands, these markings are made up of several broken lines. Complete circular markings suggest a zest for life.

Breaks When a line stops abruptly, like dashes in a sentence. Unlike forks or branches, which prompt you to look at alternatives, breaks suggest hesitation, roadblocks, obstacles. With the exception of the Girdle of Venus (which is normally composed of a series of many broken lines), breaks weaken any line's character.

Chains This type of line resembles links in a chain fence and is composed of circles, one after another. This marking weakens the impact of any line it falls on.

Clubbed thumb Thick thumbs that resemble swollen clubs or baseball bats reveal a pushy, "my way or the highway" personality. Beware of your temper! Always pushing the envelope, these folks test the limits of others, often pitting themselves against extreme odd, and sometimes risking life and limb in the process.

Cross Intersecting vertical and horizontal lines that appear on mounts or lines of the palm, usually indicating a positive character—or excess.

Depth of line The deeper the line, the more its meaning. Faintly etched Life Lines suggest poor constitution or a desperate need to be loved. Shallow Heart Lines suggest nonemotional types. Faint Head Lines suggest the need to hide your vulnerable side, even in situations that call for warmth and openness.

Double lines Also called sister lines. Double line add protection and increase the quality of the line they reflect. For example, twin Life Lines suggest good stamina and recuperation. Double Head Lines reveal an interest in literature and education. Double Heart Lines reveal a fascination with relationships, love, and sex.

Fate Line *see* Saturn Line

Fingers In palmistry, each of the five fingers represents a planet and is analyzed according to its shape, length, and smoothness of joints. For example, pronounced knuckles enhance analytical skills and denote good reasoning abilities; smooth joints demand comfort and ease in relationships and work. (Refer to each finger for more information.)

Fingertips The top phalange of the fingers. Evaluated by their shapes. Blunt-shaped tips indicate a person who doesn't grasp ideas quickly. Rounded and pointed tips indicate inspired, easy-going folks who seek emotional and intellectual gratification.

Flexibility Hands, fingers, and thumbs that gently "give" when pressure is applied to them reveal open-mindedness. A rigid hand, thumb, or fingers indicates an unyielding nature and overly traditional or conventional thinking. Overly flexible, rubbery reveal a lack of focus and trouble distinguishing between fact and fiction.

Fork A line that splits into two parts of equal length and depth, resembling a fork in the road or a branch, begs you to seek alternatives and not to believe everything you hear.

Girdle of Venus A semicircle or set of broken lines on the upper part of the palm between the Line of Heart and finger base, usually below the middle and ring fingers. Reveals a hearty appreciation of physical and sensual pleasures.

Grids Resembling a tic-tac-toe board (several small overlapping crosses), such grids diminish or embellish, depending on where they appear.

Hand shapes Wide, squarish hands suggest a love of convention, a realist, a pragmatist. Narrow or thin hands are those of dreamers and supersensitive folks.

Head Line One of the major lines. Reveals the quality of mind and intellectual appetite. Represented by the deep horizontal line starting on the inside of the palm above the thumb and above, or joined to, the beginning of the Life Line.

Heart Line One of the major lines. Reveals emotional strength. It begins below the little finger and travels horizontally, often ending beneath the index or middle fingers.

Index finger Named for the planet Jupiter, this finger indicates self-esteem and confidence. The straighter the finger, the more optimistic and decisive the individual.

Joints of the fingers Pronounced upper and lower joints reveal a more philosophical, open-minded, inquisitive nature. Large top joints enjoy figuring out what makes people and things tick; fingers with pronounced lower joints only mean increase business savvy and a sensual nature. Note: Don't confuse large joints with swelling that results from arthritis and certain medications; always ask, don't presume.

Left hand Represents your private side—your fantasies, hopes, and dreams. Lefties are known to have a more sensitive nature.

Life (or Vitality) Line One of the major lines, beginning above the thumb and traveling down toward the wrist, embracing the elevated area below the thumb (Mount of the Sun). This line reveals physical stamina and love of life, but *not* length of life.

Little finger Named for the planet Mercury (after the mythological messenger of the gods). This finger represents communication, expression, and truth. It's size, shape, and markings reveal verbal skills and business acumen.

Marriage Lines *See* Affection Lines

Mercury Line A vertical line or series of lines that run upward from the base of the palm to the mount of the little finger. Several lines suggest impatience and multifacetedness. One straight line indicates refined social skills and personal discipline.

Middle finger Named for the planet Saturn, this finger represents responsibility, duty, perseverance, and the ability to follow rules and schedules.

Moon, Mount of the The area above the wrist located at the heel or outside edge of the hand (thumbless side) that deals with imagination, the unconscious mind, and intuition.

Mounts The cushioned areas or pads below each of the fingers and on the heel of the hand. When elevated, the characteristics of that finger are emphasized; when sunken, their traits are diminished.

Nails Fingernails provide clues about temperament and personality. Shapes are judged from nail bed to the fingertip. Large square nails are slow to anger but even slower to forgive. Wide, short nails suggest narrow-mindedness and a critical nature. Long, narrow nails, like almond-shaped nails, suggest someone who prefers not to waste time with unpleasantries and who's creative but tends to sulk. Thin, narrow nails suggest someone who's quick to anger and who holds grudges.

Palm The inside area of the hand between the wrist and fingers with assorted lines. It's flipside is the back of the hand.

Palmistry Character reading gleaned from the lines and other markings on the palm, also called chiromancy.

Phalanges The three segments of the fingers (and two segments of the thumb) that comprise the joints of the fingers. The top phalange deals with intellect and concepts; the middle phalange with practical concerns; the lower phalange with instinctual and physical drives. The lower phalange of the thumb is represented by the bulbous pad beneath it, called the Mount of the Sun.

Rascelettes *See* bracelets

Right hand This hand represents what you do with your talents, how you approach the real world, and what you do with what you have.

Ring finger Named after the planet Venus (the goddess of beauty, art, and love), this finger represents happiness with occupation, hobbies, and interests.

Ring of Saturn A line or series of lines between the index and middle finger above the Heart Line encircling the middle finger. Its owner is philosophically conservative, holding on to traditional ideas and beliefs, and is not easily swayed or influenced by popular opinion or the attitudes of others.

Ring of Solomon A horizontal line or series of lines below the index finger. Its presence says your mind is always active, always seeking. Often found on the hands of teachers and writers.

Saturn Line Also called the Fate Line. A minor line that travels vertically from lower part of palm from either side of the hand toward the middle finger, often appearing broken or split or as a series of overlapping lines. It is not found on all palms. The direction and origin of this line reflects your determination to actualize hopes and dreams. The longer it is, the more you believe in yourself; when its broken or shallow, you have a need for approval and follow other's rules. You need to be constantly busy but are inclined to miss the big picture.

Size of hand Viewed in proportion to and relation to relative size of body. Large hands reveal big thinkers and those who are good with detail work; small-handed people prefer general concepts and can be somewhat stubborn.

Spatulate Refers to fingers or nails that are shaped like a Chinese fan, broader at the tip than at the base of the nail. Signifies mechanical aptitude, inventiveness, curiosity and physical energy.

Square A marking on the palm that's considered fortunate and protective. Best when located on the Mount of Jupiter, beneath the index finger.

Stars Markings found on the mounts and lines of the palm. Not to be confused with crosses, stars are composed of five or more vertical and horizontal lines in the shape of an asterisk. Stars suggest success and achievement.

Sun, Mount of the The bulbous area below the thumb embraced by the Life, or Vitality, Line. Represents your feeling for life, degree of enthusiasm and willingness to fight for what you believe.

Tassels Like fringe or a tassel on a graduate's cap, this marking generally weakens a line's quality and character.

Thumb Named after the planet Uranus, the thumb symbolizes willpower and individuality. A long, firm thumb suggests a developed ego and a highly responsible nature. Thumbs that hug the palm suggest close-mindedness.

Tone Refers to the overall "feel" of another's hand. Like a good handshake, palms that feel resilient, springy, and elastic when pressure is applied suggest good vitality and follow-through. Soft, lifeless, or flabby hands suggest laziness, lack of energy, or unreliability.

Triangles Markings that appear on mounts and lines that represent good fortune.

Venus Line A line or series of lines traveling upward from the middle of the palm to the ring finger, or *Venus*. One long straight line is best, suggesting career brilliance. Several deeply etched lines suggest personal happiness and appreciation for the arts.

Vertical line A short vertical line that resembles a parenthesis or elongated comma. When these appear on the Major and Minor Lines, vertical lines tend to impede or stifle the meaning of the line they "cut" through.

About the Author

Dennis Fairchild is a professional palmist, Tarot reader, astrologer, and psychic who lives in Michigan (the state that's shaped like a hand). His other books include *Palm Reading: A Little Guide to Life's Secrets*, *The Handbook of Humanistic Palmistry*, and *Healing Homes: Feng Shui Here and Now.*

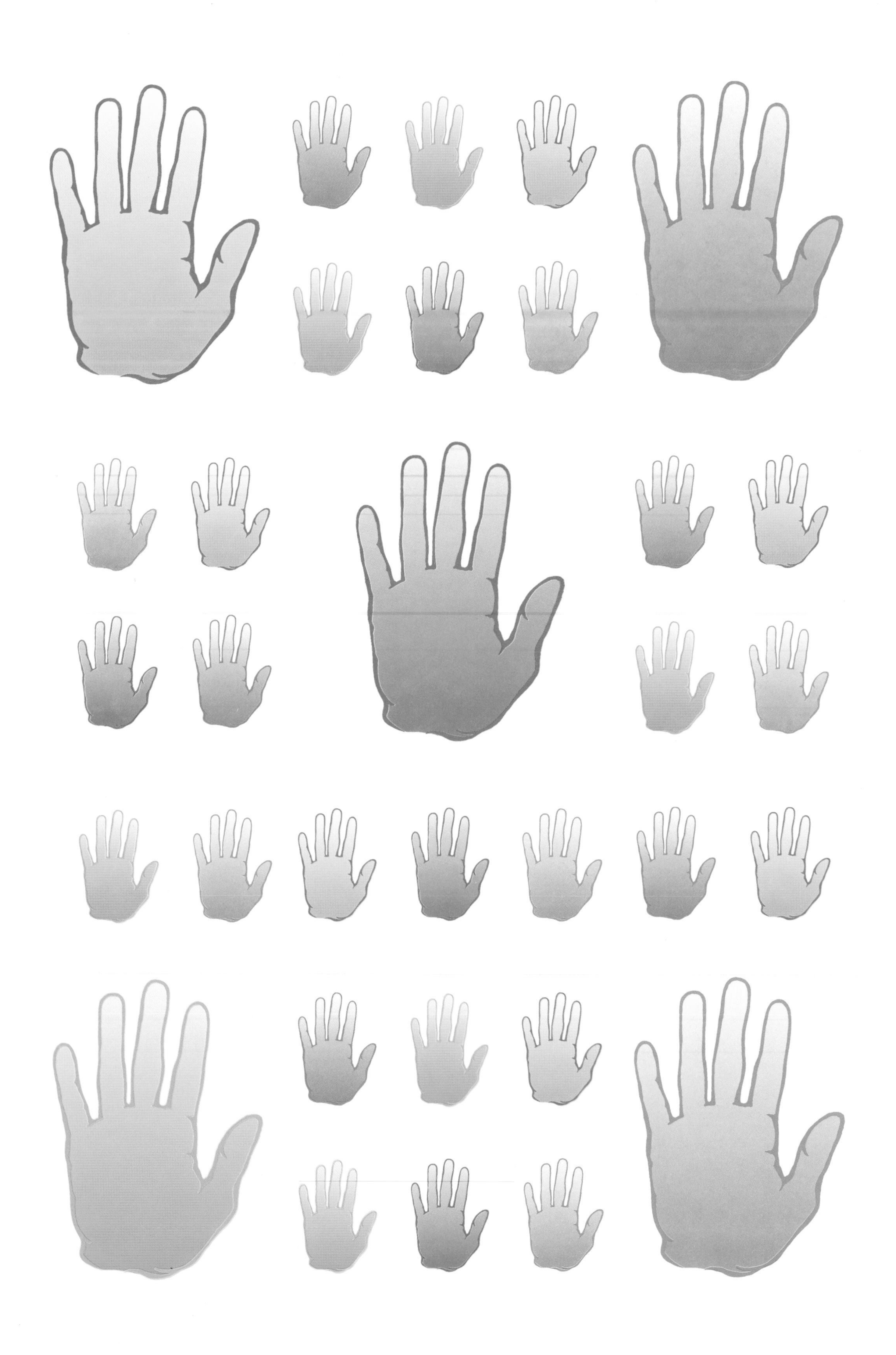